Caring Dads: Helping Fathers Value their Children

Katreena Scott, Ph.D. C. Psych.

Karen Francis, Ph.D.

Claire Crooks, Ph.D. C. Psych.

Tim Kelly, Executive Director, Changing Ways

Note for Librarians: A cataloguing record for this book is available from Library and Archives Canada at www.collectionscanada.ca/amicus/index-e.html
ISBN 1-4120-5709-4

Printed in Victoria, BC, Canada. Printed on paper with minimum 30% recycled fibre. Trafford's print shop runs on "green energy" from solar, wind and other environmentally-friendly power sources.

Offices in Canada, USA, Ireland and UK

Book sales for North America and international:
Trafford Publishing, 6E–2333 Government St.,
Victoria, BC V8T 4P4 CANADA
phone 250 383 6864 (toll-free 1 888 232 4444)
fax 250 383 6804; email to orders@trafford.com
Book sales in Europe:
Trafford Publishing (UK) Limited, 9 Park End Street, 2nd Floor
Oxford, UK OX1 1HH UNITED KINGDOM
phone 44 (0)1865 722 113 (local rate 0845 230 9601)
facsimile 44 (0)1865 722 868; info.uk@trafford.com
Order online at:
trafford.com/05-0607

10 9 8 7 6 5 4

Contents

Forward

Emerge is proud to have been one of the original pilot sites for the *Caring Dads* curriculum. Over the past five years, we have used this curriculum in 10 groups for men attending our Responsible Fatherhood Program and found it fills a giant void in addressing the particular challenges and educational needs of men with histories of domestic violence. Abusive men who are parents pose particular challenges not often met by more generic parenting education programs. For example, children of these men have often been adversely affected by their exposure to domestic violence in ways the abusers fail to recognize or misunderstand as problems of the children or their mother. More than other fathers, abusive men tend to undermine the mother's relationship with the children. The *Caring Dads* curriculum not only helps men to recognize the effects of domestic violence on their children but also provides them with positive and concrete ways to become more responsible co-parents. I particularly like *Caring Dads* emphasis on helping men recognize the importance as well as the key aspects of supporting their children's mother, whether as custodial or noncustodial fathers.

Men attending Emerge's fatherhood program include those who are simultaneously attending, or who have already completed Emerge, as well as men who are referred by courts and child welfare agencies. One unanticipated benefit of the Responsible Fatherhood Program is its ability to engage men who have not attended other abuser education programs. The *Caring Dads* curriculum provides powerful incentive for men to recognize, without being lectured or shamed, the importance of setting a more positive example for their children. In fact, an unanticipated benefit of the Responsible Fatherhood program is participants who have not attended an abuser education program sometimes decide to do so as a next step for change. Many of the men who attend the Responsible Fatherhood program have said the *Caring Dads* curriculum has not only helped them to become more caring of their children but also more responsive to the input and concerns of the mothers of their children.

David Adams, Ed.D.

Co-Director

Emerge

Acknowledgments

We would like to thank the many individuals who have helped shape this work. Since the *Caring Dads* program began, it has had amazingly generous support from a wide range of people in community and academic settings. We are deeply grateful for their contributions.

For shaping the way we think about child abuse and family violence, we would like to thank our mentors: David Wolfe, Peter Jaffe, Murray Straus, and David Finkelhor. For their contribution to thinking through the concepts and principles that form the basis of the *Caring Dads* program, we would like to thank Ted Cross and other members of the Family Violence Lab in the 2001-2002 academic year, Dan Ashbourne from the Center for Children and Families in the Justice System, Maureen Reid from the Children's Aid Society of London and Middlesex, and Angelique Jenney from the Child Development Centre in Toronto. We are also indebted to the Fathering Among Batterers Working Group, organized by Jeff Edleson and Oliver Williams, for thought-provoking discussions around how to best meet the needs of this population of men.

For assistance in the development of group material, we are thankful to those generous individuals who volunteered their time to act as co-facilitators for early *Caring Dads* groups. In particular, we wish to thank David Adams and Susan Couyote from EMERGE in Boston, Maureen Reid from the Children's Aid Society of London and Middlesex, Dan Ashbourne and Karen Bax from the Centre for Children and Families in the Justice System, and C.J. Edwards from Counterpoint Education and Counseling Cooperative in Toronto. These individuals brought a wealth of clinical experience to their work in the *Caring Dads* groups and willingly shared their time to help the program developers continue to refine group material.

We also wish to thank those who have had significant roles implementing the *Caring Dads* programs. We thank the Changing Ways (London) Inc. agency for their ongoing support. Michele Paddon also deserves significant thanks for taking on the first position as the *Caring Dads* Program Coordinator in London. With her initiative and leadership, *Caring Dads* became an established and respected service in the community. In addition, we wish to recognize Advisory Committee members from each *Caring Dads* community. These committee members have offered advice on everything from referral criteria to necessary inter-agency service agreements. We are grateful for the time and effort offered by individuals on these committees in all communities.

Finally, we wish to thank the men who have been with us through early *Caring Dads* groups for their feedback, patience, and understanding as we worked through program issues.

The production of this manual was supported, in part, by a directed donation from the United Way.

Chapter 1:

Caring Dads Gets Started

Chapter 1

Introduction

Recent years have seen a significant and welcome shift in fathers' involvement with their children. Although women are still likely to have more responsibility for children in a family, many fathers are beginning to play a more equal role. Today's fathers are involved, nurturing and active parents of their children. For most children, having a more involved father is likely to have a cascade of positive effects on their development. Children thrive with the unconditional love of adults, and when two adults are available to fulfill this role, children do better academically, socially, and emotionally. Having a strong relationship with two adults also appears to protect children from problems as they grow up. For example, when fathers are positively involved, their boys are less likely to be involved in delinquent behaviors when they are teenagers.

Unfortunately, some children do not have the benefit of a nurturing and supportive father. They may have fathers who are absent, or who terrify, belittle, isolate, reject, or ignore them. Some children have fathers who involve them in criminal activities or in adult sexual behavior. And some children live in constant anxiety about the harm that their father may cause to them, their mothers, or others they love. National child protection statistics in Canada reveal that in two-parent families, fathers are implicated as one of the perpetrators in 67% of physical abuse cases reported to authorities and in the vast majority of cases of child emotional abuse through exposure to domestic violence. Violence in the home undermines a child's safety and security and prevents children from growing to their full potential.

Our work on the *Caring Dads: Helping Fathers Value their Children* program arose from our concern for those children who cannot rely on their fathers to be non-violent. We recognized that although fathers' roles have changed, we have lagged behind in developing programs and policies that reflect this new reality. Instead, we still address, assess, and intervene mostly with mothers and children, and fail to adequately recognize the needs and responsibility of fathers. In particular, we have been failing to provide accountable services for families in which fathers have been abusive towards their children or towards their children's mothers. We developed the *Caring Dads* to help meet this need.

The following sections in this chapte tell the story of how *Caring Dads* got started. We then discuss some of the lessons that we learned as we developed the program and outline the accountability principles that now guide our work. Finally, we talk about our plans for continued improvement of the program.

How and Why *Caring Dads* Got Started

Caring Dads got its first start from an observation of Tim Kelly, one of the program authors. Tim, a longtime facilitator of groups for men who had abused their intimate partners, noticed he was seeing a second generation of violent men - sons of men who had been in past groups. He wanted to do something to help these men become better fathers and hopefully prevent their sons from yet again repeating the intergenerational cycle of violence.

Once this idea took hold, we recognized a number of other reasons to offer intervention to fathers. Perhaps most importantly, we found that in our current systems of intervention, fathers were not being held accountable for their abusive actions. Instead, women and children were being left to pick up the pieces. The example of John* and Amy is typical. John and his partner Amy had been married for 8 years and had two children, Sarah and Steve. After the birth of their second child, the relationship between John and Amy started to deteriorate. John suspected Amy of infidelity and began to interrogate her regarding her every move. When Amy refused to answer, John became more and more insistent and threatening, and on one occasion, was physically abusive to her in front of their children. John also became increasingly more impatient with the children and one night, locked Steve out of the house at 11pm as punishment. The neighbors called the police who, in turn, called child protective services.

It was at this point that the system began to fail Amy and her children. When Amy was contacted by child protective services, she was told that she needed to ensure that John did not have any contact with their children. This was difficult for Amy, who felt overwhelmed by John's insistence that he should be able to visit, Steve and Sarah's desire to see their father, and by the demands of taking care of two children by herself. Eventually Amy gave in and allowed John to come back to the house, hiding this information from her child protection worker who she was sure would disapprove. Once John returned to the home, he began to blame Amy for the fact that Sarah and Steve seemed distant from him. The children started to worry about what might happen next and began monitoring all adult conversation for indications of hostility and aggression. Amy felt sure that things were just going to get worse; however, this time she was fearful that if she called the police or child protective services, Sarah and Steve would be placed in foster care. Now she was on her own.

For us, this case emphasized how our current system of intervention fails to hold fathers accountable for their abuse of children. For example, although John was identified as the perpetrator of abuse, he was not the focus of attention at child protective services and he was not ordered to attend intervention for his fathering. Reviews of practice in child protection find that this case is fairly typical. Unfortunately, rather than engage men in treatment, most existing child welfare services either ignore the role of men in their children's lives, or identify fathers as dangerous and try to discourage father-child contact. It is the exceptional program that makes sincere efforts to engage men in redressing their abusive behavior.

The case of John and Amy also shows that by failing to intervene with men, our systems inadvertently increase the burden on women and children. For example, in this case it was Amy, rather than probation, police, or child protection, who was left with the responsibility of keeping Sarah and Steve safe from their father. Amy was also left to try to explain to her children why they were unable to see their father. When Amy was unable to meet these impossible demands, she did not feel that she could count on the system to help her. When families come to the attention of child protective services, mothers are typically held responsible for the health, safety and well-being of children, even when abusive behaviors have been perpetrated fathers or other family members.

* names and identifying details have been changed.

The Development of a Program

In considering cases like that of John and Amy we realized that problems with existing practices were only part of the problem. The other part of the problem was that there were simply no models of intervention for fathers that appropriately addressed child abuse and exposure of children to abuse of their mothers. The few programs available to fathers targeted general parenting issues. Men's overcontrolling behavior, sense of entitlement, and self-centered attitudes - all central to their abusive behavior - were not addressed. Existing programs also failed to recognize the overlap between child abuse and abuse of children's mothers, and were not organized to respond appropriately to woman victims. Intervention programs were needed that targeted men's accountability for their past and current abusive behavior and their empathy for, and understanding of, their children. (These points are further outlined in a paper we wrote. See the *Caring Dads* website (www.caringdadsprogram.com) for more information.

With these ideas firmly in mind, we began the process of developing an intervention program for abusive fathers that was eventually called: *Caring Dads: Helping Fathers Value their Children.* This 17-week group intervention aims to engage fathers, to help them develop more child-centered fathering and to take responsibility for ending their abusive behavior towards their children and their children's mothers. We offered many pilot versions of the program and with feedback from facilitators, clients, and referral agents, we made revisions and improvements. The current manual is a result of the lessons we have learned along the way. Four of the most important of these lessons are discussed below.

Lessons learned #1: Overcoming resistance to change: The importance of discussing healthy fathering before challenging abusive fathering

At the onset of our foray into program development, we understood that the men who were referred to the *Caring Dads* program were likely to be reluctant group participants. Fathers often share the societal bias towards mothers being the primary interface with social services and are likely to see services as irrelevant to them and their needs. Men who have been involved with the justice or child protection systems tend to have even more negative attitudes, and may approach any recommended intervention with hostility, anger, and defensiveness. Considerable pressure is often needed to ensure that these fathers attend intervention for long enough to give social service providers a chance to overcome men's suspicion and resistance, and develop reasonable therapeutic relationships.

Given this expected presentation, we began our first *Caring Dads* group with two sessions focused on engaging men to examine their parenting. This worked well. Then, following traditional practice in batterer intervention, we moved directly to identifying and challenging men's unhealthy and abusive parenting. We soon discovered that this was a mistake. Two sessions were simply not enough to develop sufficient trust and prepare fathers for the difficult work of critically examining their behavior. Fathers reacted with anger, hostility, defensiveness and non-attendance.

As a result of our experiences in these early groups, we decided to re-order the *Caring Dads* materials. Rather than address maltreatment first, and then build healthier models of fathering, we switched the order. This proved to be a successful modification. Now, fathers begin by considering what it means to be a good father to their children. Facilitators challenge men to get to know their children better, to become more involved, and to relate more positively to children's mothers. With this preparation, men are much more ready to hear challenges to their abusive behaviors. Now, instead of being hostile and resistant, fathers are often able to identify their unhealthy and abusive behaviors on their own, and when challenged by facilitators, they are able to more openly consider their behaviors. Admittedly, as facilitators, we sometimes struggle with the desire to immediately confront men about their harmful behaviors. However, we have confidence that delaying confrontations for a few sessions significantly improves the chances that we can successfully promote men's accountability for past actions and commitment to change.

Lessons learned #2: It is necessary to work collaboratively with other service providers to ensure that men's participation in *Caring Dads* does not have unintended negative effects on women and children, but instead has the potential to improve children's lives.

Our main purpose in offering intervention for abusive fathers has been to improve the lives of their children. Early on, we recognized that to meet this aim we needed to collaborate with and provide meaningful feedback to other community agencies. We understood that without this feedback, there was a potential for *Caring Dads* material to be misused. For example, consider the case of Alice and Stuart. When Stuart presented to the *Caring Dads* program, he and Alice were in the midst of a custody battle for their two children. Stuart was told by his lawyer that it was to his benefit to take a fathering course, as it would provide evidence of his commitment to his children. Stuart attended *Caring Dads*, but participated minimally and did not seem to be making any effort to change his fathering behavior. At the end of the program, Stuart wanted the facilitators to provide him with a certificate indicating that he had completed group.

A second example of possible misuse of the *Caring Dads* program comes from the case of Karl and Susan. Karl and Susan lived together with their four children. The family came to the attention of child protective services after allegations from the neighbors that Karl "beat" his children. These allegations were further supported by the children's history of unusual injuries. Despite the support for the allegations made, neither Susan nor the children would admit to any problems and Karl denied ever touching the children. The child protection worker referred Karl to the *Caring Dads* program and greatly reduced her monitoring of the situation.

The last example is the case of Tom, Judy and their two-year-old son, David. Tom was referred to *Caring Dads* by his Probation Officer after being convicted for assaulting David. Tom expressed genuine regret for his behavior and was eager to learn better ways to parent their very active son. He actively solicited feedback and advice from the group facilitators. However, a phone call to his partner Judy revealed that all was not as it seemed in group. Specifically, Tom was coming home from *Caring Dads* groups with lists of instructions about the things that Judy was doing wrong and was critically monitoring all of her interactions with David. Judy felt worse and worse about herself as a mother. Although she admits that they had been having difficulties, Judy felt like things were better before Tom started *Caring Dads*.

In all of these cases, there is the potential for men's participation in *Caring Dads* to have unintended negative effects on children. In the first case, there is the potential for Stuart to gain an unwarranted advantage over his partner in a custody battle; in the second, Karl may continue to abuse and silence his family; and in the third, Judy may continue to be the victim of Tom's emotionally abusive behavior. To prevent these unintended effects, the *Caring Dads* program needs to provide clear feedback to the custody assessor in Stuart and Alice's case and to the child protection worker for Karl. The *Caring Dads* program must also make contact with Judy and Susan to find out what has been happening so the men's emotionally abusive behaviors can be appropriately addressed.

Cases like these have solidified our commitment to providing feedback about men's progress in *Caring Dads*. They also resulted in the development of a number of accountability principles that we hold ourselves to in offering this program. These principles involve preparing final reports that outline men's progress towards group goals and making attempts to contact children's mothers for support and referral. We have also moved more and more towards coordinated case management (see our section on future directions), in part, due to the need to educate referral agents about appropriate follow-up assessment/observation for men who have participated in *Caring Dads* groups.

Lessons learned #3: The need for a lead agency with a feminist analysis of abuse and an appreciation of men's role as fathers

As we present information about the *Caring Dads* program to various audiences, we often feel as though we are walking along a tightrope. On one side of us are feminist researchers and women's advocates who have seen the system continually fail to meet the needs of women and children. These individuals are wary that the *Caring Dads* program represents another way that women and children are going to lose out. On the other side are a growing group of service providers and responsible fathering groups arguing that men's role as fathers have been largely ignored by the system. These individuals are wary that the *Caring Dads* program demonizes fathers and acts as a barrier to the development of more positive interventions for men.

The *Caring Dads* program treads the thin common ground between both of these groups, advocating for protection of the safety and well-being of mothers and children and for an accountable role of interventions for fathers. Given this precarious situation, it is helpful to host the *Caring Dads* program out of a lead agency that can speak to both women's and men's issues. In other words, the lead agency should have a feminist analysis of abuse, an appreciation of men's role as fathers, and credibility with agencies working for both women and men. It is not an easy job! However, there are considerable payoffs to being able to coordinate the efforts of these movements for the *Caring Dads* program and the community as a whole.

Lessons learned #4: The importance of the community

There is a fourth lesson that has been confirmed with our work on the *Caring Dads* program - that the community is a critical partner. In London Ontario, the first site for the *Caring Dads* program, there is a strong history of working together as a community to address family violence. For example, London has a long-lasting Coordinating Committee to End Woman Abuse where representatives from virtually all relevant agencies and services meet and discuss key issues.

Given the collaborative nature of the London community, a natural first step to developing and implementing the *Caring Dads* program was to form a Community Advisory Committee (CAC). This committee included members who could speak to the interests of children, women, and men. As such, it involved representatives from child protection, women's advocacy services, police, probation and parole, custody and access and family court services, as well as providers of men's, children, and families' mental health services.

The first question we asked our Community Advisory Committee was: Is the time right for a program for abusive fathers? There are a couple of reasons why a community may not be ready for a program like *Caring Dads*. One concerns the lack of essential services for ensuring the safety and well-being of victims of violence (e.g., woman's shelters). If such services do not exist, we believe that their development should take precedence over interventions to perpetrators of abuse. Another reason a community may not be ready for *Caring Dads* may concern the communication among service agencies. As we emphasized earlier, feedback loops are an essential prerequisite to ethically offering the *Caring Dads* program. If relations in a community are too strained for communication among agencies, developing these relationships should take precedence over *Caring Dads*.

Once we had established that the community was ready to offer intervention for abusive fathers, the Community Advisory Committee took on the role of guiding the program and monitoring its adherence to the overall vision. For example, it was through discussions at the Community Advisory Committee that the case coordination initiative got started (see below). The CAC also contributes to the identification and resolution of community and inter-agency level issues that arise in providing intervention and it acts as a catalyst for greater communication and information-sharing among agencies.

A specific example of the benefits of our CAC has been the development of a pool of facilitators. To run a *Caring Dads* group, facilitators need to have expertise in three areas: children's mental health and development; intervening with perpetrators of violence; and women's advocacy. Few facilitators come with all of these skills; rather, child protection workers tend to have expertise in child development and parenting; batterer counselors and women's advocates have expertise in addressing abuse, and expertise in working with men is spread amongst these and other groups. We brought this problem to our CAC and suggested that perhaps groups would work best if facilitators from different agencies joined efforts as group leaders. This idea got the support of the CAC. Each member then advocated with their home agency for the provision of in-kind donations of facilitator time to the *Caring Dads* program. Now, facilitators from a range of agencies work together with staff at the host agency to offer *Caring Dads* groups, with the side benefit of developing better inter-agency relationships.

Putting the Lessons Together: Accountability Principles for *Caring Dads*

Lessons learned over our first few years of providing *Caring Dads* groups have coalesced for us into a set of accountability principles. These principles were developed to help guide us in the many decisions that we needed to make on a day-to-day basis about how best to interact with fathers, their families, and the broader systems involved in their lives.

Accountability principles were also developed to help inform other agencies thinking of offering the *Caring Dads* program. We believe that that these guidelines on how the *Caring Dads* program should be offered are as important as the content of the intervention itself. As such, we recommend any program considering offering this service follow these accountability principles. These principles, including a questionnaire to help communities decide whether they are ready to offer an accountable program for abusive and at-risk fathers and information about a more detailed chapter outlining the rationale for these principles, can be obtained from the website (www.caringdadsprogram.com). The principles are overviewed briefly below.

Accountability to the Safety and Well-Being of Children

The first conclusion we came to is that in order to ensure *Caring Dads* is helpful to children, children's needs for safety, well-being, and stability must be given primary importance in the provision of the *Caring Dads* program. One implication of this principle is decisions regarding men's service should be guided by the needs of their children. If children are clearly too traumatized by their fathers' past abuse, or if greater involvement is likely to lead primarily to increased risk for children, then men are screened out of the *Caring Dads* program. Our commitment to children also resulted in the development of the guideline that fathers' participation in *Caring Dads* must have the potential to improve children's lives - whether men show, or fail to show, change. As previously discussed, guarding against unintended negative effects of men's participation in *Caring Dads* requires open verbal and written communication with referral sources, and the completion of clear and informative final reports. Finally, consideration of the needs of children has resulted in our choice to provide intervention primarily to men who are not seeking it voluntarily. Thus, the *Caring Dads* program developed strong collaborations with agencies that can strongly encourage or mandate men into treatment. It is only in this way that we felt able to address the needs of children in the most chronically abusive and challenging families.

Accountability to the Safety of Children's Mothers

We also recognized that children's safety, well-being and stability must be considered in the context of their families. Children are dependent on their parents, or parent figures, for the love and support necessary for healthy development and growth. When children's mothers (or other primary caregivers) are unsafe, children's needs for safety, well-being, and stability are compromised. Recognizing this interdependence, we realized that we could not, in good conscience, deal with men and their relationships with their children without also reaching out to others who had a primary role in caring for their children. We needed to assess if men were abusing other adults who were close to their children and to address these forms of abuse during *Caring Dads* groups. We also decided that to reduce the chance that men may use their participation in *Caring Dads* to inappropriately manipulate others, we would provide children's mothers with information about the program, referral to appropriate service, and if necessary, safety planning.

Responsibility to Fathers

"What about Dads?" This is a question people ask us as we talk about our concern for the safety of children and their mothers. After all, the fathers are who we see every week. Certainly, the *Caring Dads* program is also responsible to the fathers attending intervention. At a fundamental level, we believe in order to offer responsible service to men, facilitators in *Caring Dads* groups must believe that with appropriate intervention, most men can change their behavior and attitudes, and thus their relationships with their families. We have found that too often, men have been dealt with as if they cannot and will not ever change their behavior. We need to be responsive to men's distress about being judged prematurely and sensitive to men's perception of discriminatory or unfair treatment in the system, while at the same time cognizant of potential risks to children and to their mothers. We have also made it a principle to provide men with open and clear feedback when we have concerns about their behavior and about our perceptions of their progress during group. Choosing appropriate facilitators has also been important. Men often approach *Caring Dads* with high levels of anger, low motivation for change, and at time, overt hostility. To be effective, facilitators must be able to maintain a respectful and empathetic stance in the face of this presentation. Finally, we have been challenged to ensure that the *Caring Dads* program is responsive to a wide range of parenting models, and is accessible to men of diverse cultures and individual circumstances.

Accountability to the Community

Finally, we believe that the *Caring Dads* program must be accountable to the community. To facilitate community accountabilty, we recommend that the *Caring Dads* program be offered with the support, guidance, and monitoring of a Community Advisory Committee comprised of individuals who can speak to the concerns of children, women and men. We also recommend the agency offering *Caring Dads* provide community outreach and education, evaluate their program, and continue training of its own staff.

Where we are going from here: Coordinated case management

Although we have come a long way from where we started, we continue to find ways to improve what we do. Our most recent efforts to improve our program involve enhanced coordination across agencies. The starting point for our efforts was our experience with men in our groups. We often found ourselves providing feedback independently to men's probation officers, child protection workers, and community mental health workers - none of whom knew that the others existed. We also found ourselves helping men deal with conflicting orders from probation, child protection, and family court. Given the lack of coordination that existed, we decided to take on a leadership role for our clients by offering to host and facilitate coordinated case management.

At the time of writing this manual, we are in the midst of piloting a new model of inter-agency coordination. This model involves having a lead *Caring Dads* case manager compile a list of all professionals involved in men's lives and then invite them to a meeting. At this meeting, the *Caring Dads* case coordinator helps the group establish common goals for the client and develop a plan to ensure these goals are met while the client is in the *Caring Dads* group. To facilitate these steps, the *Caring Dads* case manager may provide education about the intersections of woman abuse and child abuse, the incidence of father-perpetrated child maltreatment, and the value of a healthy and nurturing father-child bond. Once a plan is set, the *Caring Dads* case coordinator is responsible for providing follow-up and follow-through with clients and other involved professionals. With this case coordination, we are confident that fewer men will fall through the cracks of our systems, and that more children will be protected.

Conclusion

As we look back over the past few years, we realize that we have come a long way from our first *Caring Dads* groups in 2001. Progress has been fast! We offer this manual as the culmination of our experiences in developing intervention to address fathers' abuse. We hope that it will help you in your attempts to better protect the safety and well-being of the children in your communities.

Chapter 2:

How to Use the *Caring Dads* Manual

Chapter 2

How to Use the *Caring Dads* Manual

Caring Dads is a group intervention program for men who have abused their children or their children's mother. *Caring Dads* has a primary commitment to the safety and well being of children. This commitment is reflected in program content and in the group process. The *Caring Dads* program emphasizes men's accountability for their behavior and helps fathers become more aware of and responsible for their use of abusive and healthy parenting strategies. A child-centered approach to fathering is advanced, where fathers are encouraged to try to recognize and prioritize their children's needs. Regardless of the stress and challenges that men are facing, facilitators assert that men must avoid using intimidating, shaming, and otherwise abusive parenting strategies. Further, men are encouraged to make choices that are responsive to their children's developmental needs. *Caring Dads* also encourages fathers to begin to appreciate the impact of child maltreatment and abuse of children's mothers and teaches men concrete skills for improving their relationships both with their children and with their children's mothers.

The *Caring Dads* manual is divided into the four major goal sections:

Goal 1. To develop sufficient trust and motivation to engage men in the process of examining their fathering

Goal 2. To increase men's awareness of child-centered fathering

Goal 3. To increase men's awareness of, and responsibility for, abusive and neglectful fathering

Goal 4. To consolidate learning, rebuild trust, and plan for the future

Each goal is comprised of a series of sessions. Labels at the bottom of each page indicate the goal and tabs on the right border of each page specify the session number, allowing facilitators to easily identify their place in the program. The goals and corresponding session titles of *Caring Dads* are listed in the following table.

Major Goals and Activities in the *Caring Dads* program

Goal 1: To develop sufficient trust and motivation to engage men in the process of examining their fathering

Session 1: Orientation	Program Overview
	Group Rules
Session 2: Considering fathering	Genograms
	Family experiences
Session 3: Developing discrepancy	My goals
	Continuing to develop discrepancy

Goal 2: To increase men's awareness of child-centered fathering

Session 4: Child-centered fathering	Continuum of parenting behavior
	Responsive and unresponsive praise
Session 5: Building relationships with our children	Review of praise
	How well do you know your kids?
Session 6: Listening to children	Listening to children
	Relationship building challenges
Session 7: Fathers as part of families	Setting a good example
	Appreciation for my children's mother
Session 8: Eliminating barriers to better relationships	The connections between thoughts, feelings and actions
	Thoughts and beliefs to watch out for
Session 9: How are children different from adults?	Understanding child development
	Practical applications

Goal 3: To increase men's awareness of, and responsibility for, abusive and neglectful fathering behaviors and their impact on children

Session 10: Recognizing unhealthy, hurtful, abusive and neglectful fathering behaviors	The other end of the continuum: child maltreatment
	A closer look at emotional abuse
Session 11: How am I responding to my children's needs?	Emotional abuse and neglect as forms of abuse
	Problem-solving for parents exercise
Session 12: Relationship with my child's mother	Problem-solving for parents continued
	What children learn from abusive and controlling fathering
Session 13: Problem-solving in difficult situations	Abuse of children's mothers
	Problem-solving for parents continued
Session 14: Decreasing denial and minimization	Shame and secrecy
	Effect of denial on children
	Problem-solving for parents continued

Goal 4: Consolidating learning, rebuilding trust, and planning for the future

Session 15: Rebuilding trust and healing	Taking responsibility for the past and moving into the future
	Rebuilding trust
Session 16: What about discipline?	Summarizing alternatives to punishment
	Defining discipline
Session 17: Wrapping up	Review of main concepts
	Where am I going from here?

The organization of material for *Caring Dads* sessions has been designed for ease of use. Each session begins with a single page summary table that briefly outlines the exercises for that session. On the following pages, in-depth descriptions of sessions and activities are provided. These descriptions all follow a similar format, as shown below.

Session 8: Eliminating barriers to better relationships

Goal: To increase men's awareness of child-centered fathering

⟹ First, a summary is provided of the main goal and themes of the session.

Theme: This session, men begin to focus more closely on negative fathering behaviors. The session begins by providing men with time for a longer check-in ….

Materials Required for Session 8

- Worksheet: Thoughts, feelings, and actions triangle
- Worksheet: Thoughts and beliefs to watch out for

⟹ Next, facilitators are provided with a list of materials that they will need for that session.

Exercise 1: Connections between thoughts, feelings and actions (30 minutes)

Explain that one step to becoming a better father is to better understand how things go wrong. This is what we are going to …..

Have the group brainstorm a list of the father's feelings at the beginning point...

⟹ Then, suggested exercises are outlined, with specific instructions on how material may be presented and with suggestions for how facilitators may best process the material in group.

Process notes, cautions, etc.

Men tend to think that behavior is the easiest angle of the triangle to change. In other words, they may believe that the best way to change is to simply decide...

⟹ Helpful hints about facilitating exercises are provided as process notes, cautions, etc. See below for more information.

Homework

For homework this week, men are asked to track their thoughts in difficult situations….

⟹ Finally, facilitators are provided with a set of worksheets to be used for homework.

Notes are made throughout sessions of helpful therapeutic strategies, cautions, and possible follow-up exercises. A variety of formatting conventions and symbols are used to help guide facilitators' reading. These are specifically described below.

PROCESS NOTES PROCESS NOTES alert facilitators to issues that commonly arise while presenting specific exercises. These notes provide helpful strategies for addressing these issues. Process notes are as important as content notes for successfully presenting an exercise.

 The CAUTION sign is used to alert facilitators to issues that have the potential to disrupt the group process. Facilitators should be alert to these cautions and work to prevent or intervene immediately in these situations.

 The DECISION POINT icon highlights sections in which a choice of material is offered for use. Facilitators may choose the most appropriate exercise depending on the needs, living situations, and presenting issues of the majority of their *Caring Dads* group.

 Most of the exercises in *Caring Dads* are written with a primary focus on men's abuse of their children. This icon marks recommendations for modifying and adapting exercises to the needs of FATHERS WHO PRESENT PRIMARILY WITH ABUSE OF THEIR CHILDREN'S MOTHERS.

 The IF TIME icon identifies follow-up options to various exercises that can help facilitators take advantage of occasions when groups progress through exercises quickly. These follow-up options are additions to the main program, and should be used only if there is excess time in group.

Considerations in Group Planning and Delivery

There are a number of organizational details that need to be addressed prior to beginning a first *Caring Dads* group. Listed below are guidelines for two critical steps in group planning: establishing eligibility and developing a program agreement. In addition, guidance is provided for choosing facilitators and writing final reports.

Program Eligibility

One of the first tasks for communities planning to offer *Caring Dads* is to decide which men are eligible for referral to the program. Men's eligibility for program participation may be influenced by a variety of factors including their risk for perpetrating abuse, referral source, legal involvement and participation in other treatment programs. The following is a list of questions to help communities develop a reasonable set of criteria. A sample Program Eligibility Criteria form is included in Appendix B. In general, the Advisory Committee is involved in determining the eligibility criteria appropriate for that community. We recommend inviting approximately 15 to 20 eligible men to *Caring Dads* groups. In our experience, with this number of invited men, a final group size of 8 to 12 will be achieved.

Questions to consider in determining eligibility

- What level of risk for abuse is appropriate for men's participation? Should men be accepted only if they have been charged with, or are under investigation for, child abuse or neglect? Only if they are referred by another professional? Should men who approach the program voluntarily be offered service?

- If men are accepted into the program without a referral from a professional, how will they be screened for eligibility? To whom will feedback be provided about their progress? Provision of feedback is an especially important question if men are also involved in custody and access disputes.

- Will men with a history of perpetrating child sexual abuse be accepted into the program? Under what conditions?

- Will men with particular diagnoses (e.g., antisocial personality disorder) or other comorbid problems (e.g., alcohol dependence) be screened out?

- Will the program support referrals for clients speaking the non-majority language? If so, how will interpretation and homework support be provided?

- How much contact do men need to have with their children to be eligible for the program? Will men be accepted if they are allowed only supervised access to their children? What about men who are prohibited from contacting their own children, but are regular caregivers for other children?

- Are men eligible for participation regardless of their status in the legal system? What if they have outstanding charges for child abuse?

- Are men eligible if they are involved in custody and access proceedings? Will they be accepted if they are currently pursuing changes in custody and/or access? What if they are involved in prolonged custody and access battles with no current court action? Will men only be eligible if custody and access arrangements are stable and non-problematic?

- Will men be accepted if they are concurrently involved in other services, such as intervention for domestic violence, alcohol or drug use, or individual therapy? What conditions will govern communicaiton men's involvement in concurrent services?

- Will men need to have a minimal level of acknowledgment of their past abusive behavior?

The right answers to these questions will vary for each community. These questions are provided to help Advisory Committees consider key issues.

Program agreements

It is crucial to be open and honest with men about the conditions and limitations of their involvement in the *Caring Dads* program. To ensure that men understand the guidelines that govern their involvement in *Caring Dads*, we strongly recommend that programs develop a Service Agreement. This agreement can then be given to men as a reference and reviewed with them during their first *Caring Dads* session. Key issues for this agreement are:

Confidentiality. Men should be informed of the limits of confidentiality in the *Caring Dads* group.

Communication. Men should be informed of the frequency and nature of information sharing that will occur between group co-facilitators and men's referral agents. Men should be told these reports will be written on their progress during group and shared with their referral agents. Men also need to be informed of the program's policies for contacting and sharing information with children's mothers.

Evaluation of progress. Men need to be aware that their progress in group will be evaluated on the basis of their participation and change, and not based solely on their attendance.

Conditions of involvement. Finally, men need to be informed of the conditions of their involvement in the group. For example, men need to be informed of the number of groups they may miss and of the rules governing their behavior during and between group sessions (e.g., we typically assert that men may not come to group if they have been drinking or using drugs the day of group).

Similar to the eligibility criteria, the Service Agreement can be constructed with the input of the Advisory Committee and based on the specific needs and agreements of the community. For illustrative purposes, a sample Service Agreement is provided in Appendix B.

Co-Facilitator Considerations

We recommend that a team of two or three co-facilitators offer the *Caring Dads* program. The following guidelines offer a summary of those aspects of co-facilitator knowledge and experience that we have found most important.

Firm knowledge of child development, woman abuse and working with men

The *Caring Dads* program spans three traditionally separated service areas: child services, women's advocacy, and intervention for men. Because it is unusual for one individual to have knowledge and experience in all of these domains, two (or more) facilitators' combined knowledge is likely needed. We recommend that, as a group, the facilitators possess the following:

Knowledge of child development. The facilitator team should have knowledge of child development and parent-child relationships. With this knowledge, facilitators can provide education about the developmental capacities of children, offer advice to fathers about age-appropriate strategies for developing better parent-child relationships, and make distinctions between "good enough" parenting and parenting strategies that are potentially abusive or neglectful.

Understanding of the dynamics of woman abuse. Many of the men in *Caring Dads* groups have been abusive towards both their children and their children's mothers. To deal with this appropriately, at least one group facilitator should have knowledge and experience in women's advocacy. This facilitator can offer knowledge of common patterns of abuse, expertise in sorting though the conflicting stories of men and women, and can help ensure that the group responds appropriately to instances of abuse of children's mothers.

Experience working with men. It is important that one of the facilitators has experience working with men, preferably male perpetrators of family violence. Facilitators experienced in working with perpetrators will offer skill in building rapport with resistant clients, challenging men's abusive behaviors, and in considering the unique challenges faced by fathers in society.

Training in cognitive-behavioral therapy. Finally, *Caring Dads* groups will benefit from having at least one facilitator trained in doing cognitive-behavioral group therapy. This facilitator can offer leadership in the third section of the program during which men's abusive behaviors, and abuse-supporting cognitions, are directly targeted for change.

At least one male and one female co-facilitator

We recommend that *Caring Dads* groups be offered by a team of at least one male and one female co-facilitator. Female facilitators can help counter men's negative views of women and can offer a model of parenting that differs from the negative experiences that men may have experienced as children. Male facilitators can provide men with a sense of comfort in early sessions and a role model with whom to identify. Finally, as a team, a male and female co-facilitator are able to model equalitarian gender relationships.

Professional qualifications

Because the *Caring Dads* program is offered at the intersection of child welfare, justice, and mental health systems, an unusually large number of ethical issues can arise. In particular, issues of confidentiality and dual roles are common. Professional training in a counselling field provides the knowledge, guidelines, and professional skills for resolving such ethical issues. Moreover, involvement in a professional society offers counselors ready access to continued knowledge and skill development though professional association newsletters and conferences. For these reasons, we recommend that when possible, programs hire *Caring Dads* facilitators with professional qualifications.

Writing final reports

To ensure that the *Caring Dads* program is accountable to the safety and well being of children, we believe it is necessary to write a clear and well-conceptualized final report for each *Caring Dads* client. Although time consuming, these reports are critical for providing the broader child protection, justice, and mental health systems with the feedback (positive and negative) necessary for making better decisions about children's needs. Certificates of group completion or group participation checklists fall short of this goal.

In writing final reports, we recommend that facilitators focus on direct examples of men's accountability, responsibility, attitudes, and reported behavior. Clear and detailed case notes of men's progress through sessions are very helpful for this purpose. Our reports include a summary of why each man was referred to the program, a description of his contact with his children, his record of attendance and participation, and his progress through the program. In considering men's progress, we make reference to the four major goals of the *Caring Dads* program; in particular, we comment specifically on clients' progress, and lack of progress towards: 1) engagement and openness to change; 2) development of child-centered fathering; 3) accountability for abuse; and 4) ability to rebuild a trusting relationship with their children. Finally, we make recommendations about other services that may be helpful for clients. Sample reports are available through the password protected portion of the website (www.caringdadsprogram.com).

Videos

Facilitators of *Caring Dads* need to be aware up front of difficulties with videos. In four *Caring Dads*, sessions 8, 10, 11 and 12, we suggest using videos for educating men in exercises or exercise options. Videos are not provided as part of this manual, mostly due to the prohibitive expense of getting the rights to distribute copyrighted materials. Due to our difficulties making video material available, we considered omitting video education altogether. Feedback from our facilitators convinced us otherwise. It was generally agreed that the videos were valuable to helping men understand the types of behaviors that we were addressing. We suggest that if your program is going to offer the *Caring Dads* program that you take a look at videos that you already have for relevant clips. In addition, we are trying to keep a list of relevant videos on the *Caring Dads* website as a resource for program providers.

Additional notes on manual use

We recommend that for the first few times though the *Caring Dads* program, facilitators stick as closely as possible to the program as outlined. The current organization and choice of exercises is a result of considerable trial and error and detailed feedback from our facilitators and clients. However, once facilitators have a good sense of the program and a clear understanding of the overall goals of the *Caring Dads* program, we encourage flexibility. The following section provides suggestions for flexible planning. It is intended primarily for those facilitators who have already run one or two cycles of the *Caring Dads* group and who feel comfortable with the overall content and process.

An alternate way of using this manual: Goal by goal

One way to incorporate flexibility into the *Caring Dads* program is to organize group activities according to men's progress through the four therapeutic goals. In other words, rather than devote a particular number of sessions to a specific goal, the group can remain on a particular topic until the goal is achieved for all group members. For example, facilitators may decide to devote five or six sessions to engagement (rather than the suggested three) to ensure that all men are engaged and ready to progress to the second goal. This strategy of service is inevitably more time-consuming, but may also better serve the needs of those clients who are most vulnerable to failure.

Additional and alternate exercises

We are aware that there are a large variety of exercises that can be used to reach the goals of the *Caring Dads* program and that the needs of individual groups differ considerably. Facilitators who are familiar with *Caring Dads* should feel free to substitute or add exercises to the program. To aid in this process, the password protected area of the *Caring Dads* website includes a list of alternate exercises. In addition, we encourage facilitators to share positive exercise adaptations or substitutions by sending a description of the exercise to the website where it can be posted for other facilitators to see and consider. In this way, everyone's practice can improve!

Shortened program

The *Caring Dads* program has been designed so men can enter the group without prior group experience. A single father with issues around child abuse, for example, may come to the *Caring Dads* program without prior experience in a batterer intervention or a parenting program. If *Caring Dads* is offered as an adjunct to another program such that men begin group with high levels of change motivation and an understanding of the dynamics of abuse in their lives, a shortened 12-week program may be considered. In this case, we recommend offering the following 12 sessions:

Session 2: Considering fathering

Session 4: Child-centered fathering

Session 5: Building relationships with our children

Session 6: Listening to children

Session 7: Fathers as part of families

Session 8: Eliminating barriers to better relationships

Session 9: How are children different from adults?

Session 10: Recognizing unhealthy, hurtful, abusive and neglectful fathering behaviors

Session 11: How am I responding to my children's needs

Session 12: Problem-solving in difficult situations

Session 13: Relationship with my child's mother

Session 16: What about discipline?

GOAL 1:

To develop sufficient trust and motivation to engage men in the process of examining their fathering

General Notes

Goal 1: To develop sufficient trust and motivation to engage men in the process of examining their fathering

The main therapeutic goal of the first three sessions of *Caring Dads* is *to develop trust and engagement so that men can be challenged.* This goal recognizes men may not feel they need to make any changes to their parenting. Developing trust and engaging men is the first step towards helping them realize they may benefit from learning to relate to their children in new ways. To help men develop motivation for intervention, they are encouraged to explore the difference, and the potential for difference, between the way they father and the fathering they experienced as children. Counsellers should anticipate men often have mixed or negative feelings about their attendance at group, and should remain open to having men voice their concerns about attending group or about the program's approach. Men's sharing in these initial sessions also forms the building blocks for developing group cohesion.

Key therapeutic skills for this section include:

1. Modeling respect

Men will be sharing personal information throughout the group sessions. Initially, these disclosures involve sharing their varied and often complex family histories. To allow men to do this safely, and to foster their motivation to continue sharing, counselors should highlight the importance of demonstrating respect for others by mentioning and modeling respect, and by supporting men's respectful behaviors.

2. Non-defensive responding to men's challenges

The majority of men are likely to experience at least some reservations about their attendance at group. Some men may raise their concerns and directly challenge facilitators within session, while others may show their concern non-verbally. Facilitators should anticipate some discussion of men's difficulties and respond to men's concerns in a non-confrontational and non-defensive manner. The following are some common challenges and potential responses:

a. "I don't belong here."

When a man says this, facilitators may wish to respond by pointing out some difficulty resulted in the man attending the program, and he will gain the most by focusing on the opportunity to learn something from the program. Alternatively, they could make a neutral comment about the fact that over the next several weeks the group will be discussing a great deal of information about children and parenting, and every member of the group will likely find at least a couple of useful pieces of information.

b. "Child protective services (or other referral agent) had no right to make me come here."

A response similar to that outlined previously may be used for this challenge. With respect to child protective services, counselors can emphasize that these services are often complex to navigate. They can tell men that the group will be able to discuss ways to better communicate with child protective services and to work with the child protection system for the well-being of their children.

c. "The problem isn't me, it's my child/child's mother."

In response to this challenge, facilitators should indicate that the group focus is on that which group members can control – their own behavior, rather than the behavior of others. Again, facilitators may wish to encourage men to consider the program as an opportunity to improve their relationship with their children and families.

3. Moving from generalities to specifics

When discussing their experiences, men often speak in generalities (e.g., when describing his experiences of being fathered, a man may say that his father "was a good dad"). Counselors should encourage men to begin identifying specifics (i.e., "What did it mean to be a good father?"). This guidance towards being more specific will help prepare men for doing careful examination of their own experiences, thoughts, feelings and behaviors. In addition, by asking for concrete examples, counselors can be assured everyone has the same understanding, or at the very least, reveal differences in people's working definitions.

4. Avoiding confrontation

The initial sessions are focused on fostering trust and engagement, and enhancing motivation for intervention. Thus, counsellors should avoid confrontation and instead focus on building the relationships and group cohesiveness necessary to use confrontation effectively in later sessions. For example, a client may seek to start a power struggle over a controversial issue such as spanking. Rather than engaging in a debate at this early stage, counsellors should try to defer the discussion. It is particularly important to avoid moralistic language that the men may perceive as judgmental. Instead, comments such as, "We really aren't here to make judgments – we want to talk about ways to improve your relationship with your child" may help diffuse the situation.

5. Developing discrepancies between men's desired outcomes and their actions

When men enter group, they often cannot see the connection between their actions and the negative responses that they are getting from their children. Guiding men to identify discrepancies between their actions and their desired outcomes will foster motivation.

6. Encouraging men to give feedback to each other

The men in the group are an important resource to each other. Thus, early in the program they should be encouraged to work together. By giving feedback respectfully to each other and recognizing some shared experiences, men's sense of isolation may be reduced, and a sense of belonging or group cohesiveness can develop.

Session 1: Orientation

Goal: To develop sufficient trust and motivation to engage men in the process of examining their fathering

Exercises and Handouts	Content of Exercise
Introductions (10 min)	Facilitators and men briefly introduce themselves. More in depth introductions will occur next week.
Program Overview (70 minutes) Refer to Program Agreement	Briefly review group content and outline policies and procedures, such as limits to confidentiality. Give men a chance to voice their concerns about being part of the group. Discuss the appropriateness of men talking about group with their children.
Establishing Group Rules * Refer to Group Rules (20 min)	Establish rules for confidentiality and respect and practical rules around attendance and punctuality.
Checkout (10 min)	If the group has gone well, invite men to checkout with their thoughts and feelings about having been through the first session. Facilitators should support pro-group attitudes.

Session 1: Orientation

Goal: To develop sufficient trust and motivation to engage men in the process of examining their fathering

Theme: The purpose of this session is to introduce men to the content and nature of the *Caring Dads* group. These tasks can be done as the first week of the group, or as an information session prior to the group being started. The tone of this session tends to be business-like as a major aim is to provide men with information.

Materials Required for Session 1

• Copies of Service Agreement

• Copies of Program Rules

Introductions (10 min)

Facilitators and men should introduce themselves to the group. Men may also be asked to comment on how they are feeling at this beginning point. Common feelings are nervousness, annoyance, and resentment at being referred to the program. Some men are able to articulate a sense of hope that being involved in a program will improve their relationship with their children.

Introductions during this session should be brief. More in depth introductions that include asking about other members of men's families will occur next week.

Program Overview (70 min)
See Service Agreement Sample (Appendix B)

Briefly review the basic content of *Caring Dads* and outline policies and procedures, such as limits to confidentiality. A sample service agreement is provided for consideration in Appendix B.

Most of the time, men will be coming to *Caring Dads* without a clear understanding of the topics to be covered or the role of the group. For many, this group will be their first experience in a therapeutic setting. It is important for facilitators to be straightforward about the work that will be undertaken. In addition, facitlitators are encouraged to give men the opportunity to question and challenge the material presented. Here are some points that should be covered:

1. Facilitators should let men know the group will talk about:

   • ways for men to improve their relationships with their children and families

   • children's needs and the ways that children develop

   • the effect of different parenting behaviors (both positive and negative) on children

2. Men should also be informed that during this group, they will be challenged to closely examine their relationships to try to figure out what role their behavior has played in leading to their referral to *Caring Dads*.

3. Let men know that the work done in *Caring Dads* is difficult, and that facilitators will sometimes be asking them to consider things that they prefer to avoid thinking about or discussing.

4. Some men in the group will have conflictual relationships with their children's mothers. It is important to set the expectation that men will not use material from this group to coerce or abuse children's mothers or their children. Facilitators should inform men that group material should be used to help men improve themselves, not others.

5. Discuss policy and procedures around confidentiality, information sharing and mandated reporting.

6. Introduce the concept of homework assignments and why they are important. Let men know that homework will take approximately half an hour to complete and should be done during the week between sessions. Encourage men to put aside a consistent time during the week to complete homework exercises.

   Men should also be told to bring their homework with them every week. Bringing the homework to group is important because at various times, the group will review homework exercises from past weeks. Homework is also important because it is one of the ways that facilitators can assess men's progress in *Caring Dads* and provide an accurate report of their progress back to referral sources.

7. Address whether men should discuss group material with their children. It is very important that men understand that children are vulnerable to feeling blamed and guilty for their father's negative feelings. For this reason, facilitators should encourage men who are thinking about sharing group material with their children to discuss it with a group facilitator beforehand. In response to children's general questions about where men are going, facilitators may recommend that men tell their children that they are coming to a group to improve their parenting.

Throughout this discussion, encourage men to ask questions and comment on the material being presented.

> **PROCESS NOTES:**
>
> *It is particularly important that men be given the opportunity to voice their concerns about being referred to Caring Dads. Men may feel that their referral was unfair or that they have been victimized by the system. Facilitators' ability to respond non-defensively to men's challenges is critical to engaging men and to modelling respect. Group leaders should use reflective listening skills to validate men's feelings without getting drawn into debating the veracity or justice of men's situations. They should follow-up with comments about the potential value of men thinking through their circumstances in different and possibly more helpful ways, as will be done throughout the Caring Dads program.*

PROCESS NOTES CONTINUED:

It is important for facilitators to maintain control of the group process while allowing men to air their concerns. Some signs that the group process is becoming counter-therapeutic may include:

- *Men talking over each other*
- *Participants all agreeing emphatically with one member or on an issue*
- *Men beginning to challenge facilitators to support the opinion of one of the men in the group*

Should facilitators determine that the group process is becoming problematic, they should intervene by:

- *Ensuring that one person speaks at a time*
- *Continuing to reflect men's feelings - it is important to not engage in a power struggle and act in a defensive manner*
- *Bringing men back to the difficulties that they find themselves in. Facilitators can do this by acknowledging men's anger, but asserting that men still have control over their perception of the situation. For example, facilitators may comment: "I hear that you are feeling quite frustrated, but I wonder what that feeling is doing for you, and whether there may be a better way to go about dealing with this situation." Or they might say: "I hear what you are saying, but I also know that something must not be working, or else you wouldn't be in this group."*

As men air concerns about being referred to this group, facilitators should try to help them move from a position of attending group merely in compliance with an order or referral (often with the expectation that group attendance alone will be sufficient to satisfy their referral source), to a more genuine commitment to change. Facilitators should emphasize that evaluation of men's progress will be based on their participation and change, not merely their attendance. Facilitators can also emphasize that parenting is difficult, and men seldom get the opportunity to talk about fathering issues. If men are merely "doing time" in group, they are missing this opportunity to learn from each other.

Concerns With Policies for Contacting Children's Mothers

Prior to the group beginning, the agency responsible for the *Caring Dads* program (in conjunction with the Community Advisory Committee) will have delineated policies for attending to the safety of children's mothers. Most often, the commitment to addressing partner safety involves contacting children's mothers directly. Facilitators should acknowledge men might have specific concerns due to their unique situations and advise men they will have an opportunity to discuss it one-on-one in their intake interview. Give the example that if men are single fathers with sole custody, contact would not be made with children's mothers.

Complaints About Children's Mothers

Be aware that a number of the men in the room may be referred as a result of assaulting their partners. These men may present with many complaints about the way their children's mothers parent. Assert that the purpose of *Caring Dads* is to address men's issues, not to struggle against something that group members can't control - the choices of other people.

Establishing Group Rules (20 min)
See Group Rules Sample (Appendix B)

It is important to begin any group by establishing ground rules for confidentiality and respect, and practical rules around attendance and punctuality. With this particular client group, it is often most efficient to present the rules and then allow comment. This exercise should also help men transition from focusing on their concerns about being in this program to focusing on material to be presented.

A sample set of group rules is provided in Appendix B. These rules may differ from site to site. Facilitators should ensure that men have a copy of these rules for reference.

> **PROCESS NOTES:**
>
> *Facilitators should use their judgment about their degree of flexibility with these rules. Most of the time, the rules as presented are not problematic. However, it is useful to engage men in a discussion of their agreement and disagreement with these rules and to give them some control over the process. For example, in past groups, modifications have been made to rules regarding lateness or the number of weeks that men can miss.*

Checkout (10 min)

As a final exercise, facilitators can have each man check out with how he is feeling about the meeting. Most of the time, men will respond with feelings of relief and with greater comfort in the group process. Facilitators should reinforce men's feelings of engagement and any comments that men have made that are pro-group or pro-change.

What if Men are Still Angry?

If facilitators have spent the majority of group time dealing with hostility from one or two men, they may wish to ensure that these men check out last. Choose the seemingly most pro-group man first, and he will set a precedent for others. If facilitators are very concerned that men will check out only with hostility and anger, they may wish to skip this exercise and work on a plan to address men's feelings during the next group. It is important to end the group on a positive or neutral note. For example, facilitators may reiterate the hope that each participant will find something useful in the weeks to come.

Session 2: Considering Fathering

Goal: To develop sufficient trust and motivation to engage men in the process of examining their fathering

Exercises and Handouts	Content of Exercise
Exercise 1: Creation of Genograms (40 min)	Have men do in depth introductions of themselves by telling the group about their families (i.e., how many children, their ages, their living situation). Create a genogram for each man and post it on the group walls.
Exercise 2: Family Experience and Patterns (50 minutes)	Create two columns on the board and label them "What would you like to do the same as your father?" and "What would you like to do differently than your father?" Brainstorm lists for both columns. End this exercise by emphasizing that by participating in *Caring Dads*, men are taking first steps to improving their parenting.
Homework Assignment (10 min)	Have men write down three hopes they have for their relationships with their children.
Checkout (10 min)	Invite men to check out with their thoughts and feelings about the session.

Session 2: Considering Fathering

Goal: To develop sufficient trust and motivation to engage men in the process of examining their fathering

Theme: In this session, facilitators continue to engage men by helping them develop a better understanding of their families. Facilitators encourage men to begin to consider their own experiences of being fathered, and to identify aspects of their experience they do and do not want to repeat. In doing these activities, facilitators invite men to take responsibility for becoming better fathers for their children.

Materials Required for Session 2

- Large pieces of paper to record men's genograms and tape to post them

Exercise 1: Creation of Genograms (40 min)

Ask men to describe their children and their children's families. Create a genogram for each family. Sometimes these individual genograms take a long time to complete. If men seem restless, acknowledge that it takes a lot of time, but underscore the importance of the activity.

The following page provides a description of conventions typically used in genograms. There are symbols to denote the family members and to capture the relationships among family members.

Facilitators may want to add notes to genograms to clarify details. For example, if a child is in foster care during the week but home on weekends, this arrangement can be noted on the diagram.

Genograms should be posted on group walls each week as a reminder to co-facilitators and to other group members of the names, ages, and living situations of all men's children and their children's mothers. Facilitators can also invite men to bring pictures to add to their genograms, which will be returned to them at the end of the program.

Genogram Conventions

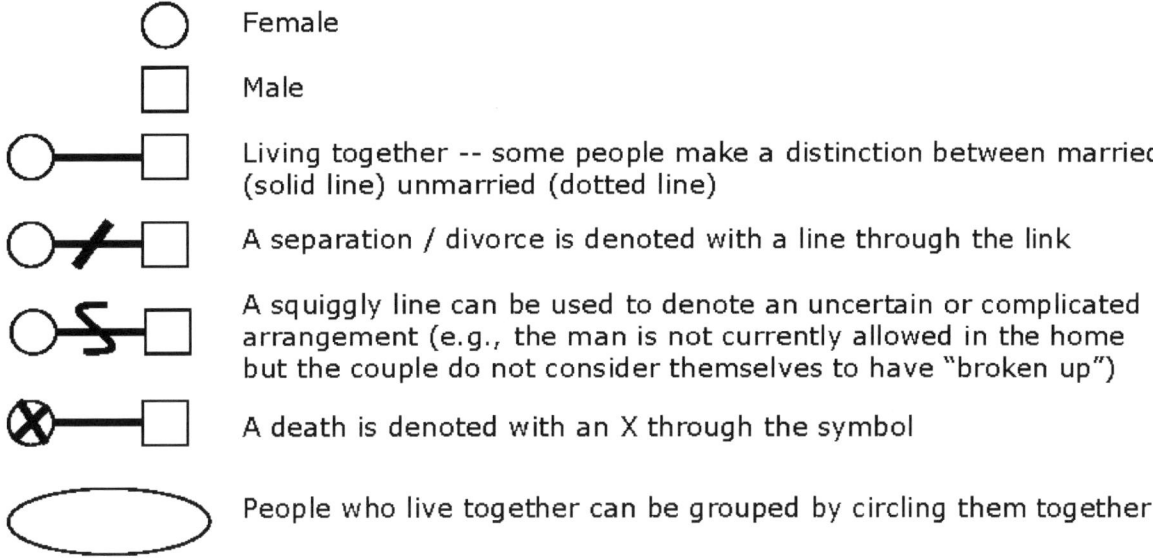

○ Female

□ Male

○—□ Living together -- some people make a distinction between married (solid line) unmarried (dotted line)

○╫□ A separation / divorce is denoted with a line through the link

○〜□ A squiggly line can be used to denote an uncertain or complicated arrangement (e.g., the man is not currently allowed in the home but the couple do not consider themselves to have "broken up")

⊗—□ A death is denoted with an X through the symbol

⬭ People who live together can be grouped by circling them together

Other important notations for children are show below:

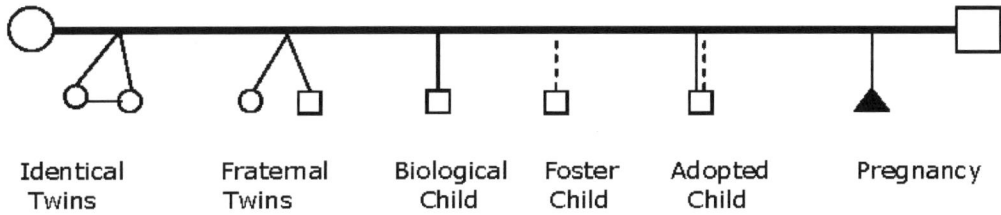

Identical Twins	Fraternal Twins	Biological Child	Foster Child	Adopted Child	Pregnancy

Example: Juan and Kathy have two children, Serena (age 4) and Tomas (age 2). In addition, Juan was married before (to Louisa) and there is one child from that relationship (Linda, age 14). Juan, Kathy, and their two children reside together.

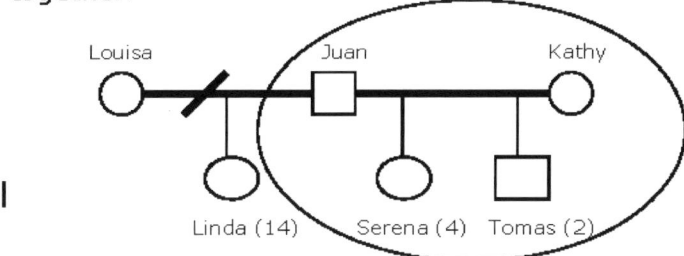

Exercise 2: Family Experiences and Patterns (50 min)

Introduce this exercise by explaining much of what we believe and do is learned from people we are close to and we tend to learn our parenting from our own families and the experiences that we had as children. Facilitators should explain that change begins by having men think about the things that they learned from their fathers and how these lessons might be influencing the way they parent their children.

Create two columns on the board and label them "What would you like to do the same as your father?" and "What would you like to do differently than your father?" Men who did not grow up with a father are asked to think about who they may have learned fathering from (e.g., uncles, grandfathers, foster fathers). Have men brainstorm a list of things that they would like to do the same and like to do differently than their own fathers, and write them in the appropriate column.

Be sure to ask for specifics. For example, if a man reports that his father was too strict and that he doesn't want to be that way, facilitators should ask him for an example of a time that his father was too strict. Facilitators should aim to have each of the men contribute at least one comment in the facilitated discussion as it will set a precedent for them to do so in future sessions.

Invite men to consider whether this exercise has led them to any new goals for them for improving their fathering. End this exercise by emphasizing that by participating in this group, men are taking first steps to improving their relationships with their children.

If There is Time Left Over

Option 1:

Once the group as a whole has brainstormed a list of things they do and do not want to do the same as their fathers, pair men up. Have them share with their partner one or two good things they learned and one or two things they would rather not have learned from their fathers. This work in pairs provides a chance for individual processing and also starts to build group cohesion. It may also be a way for men who are more anxious about speaking out in front of the larger group to get to know other group members.

Option 2:

An alternate follow-up exercise is to have men generate responses to the question, "What expectations do you have for yourself as a father?" This follow-up can be used to:

- Emphasize discrepancies between men's childhood experiences and their desires for their relationships with their children

- Gently challenge instances where there should be more discrepancy between men's reports of their experience as children and their current aims as fathers

- Explore differences in the expectations of fathers over time, or in different cultural contexts

- Acknowledge that other people may have different expectations of men and that men may feel pressured as a result of these differences

Homework (10 min)
Worksheets available in Appendix A

For homework, men are asked to identify three hopes they have for their relationships with their children. If desired, facilitators can begin this exercise during group by having men brainstorm a list of hopes men might have for their relationships.

> *PROCESS NOTES:*
>
> *Research indicates interventions that include a homework component tend to be more successful in changing behavior than those that do not. In addition, men's completion of homework is one source of information facilitators can use to assess men's progress. For these reasons, we strongly encourage that facilitators take men's completion (or non-completion) of homework very seriously.*
>
> *To establish good homework norms, facilitators can check men's homework at the beginning of sessions. This protocol is not to encourage facilitators to be rigid, but rather to ensure that positive expectations are set with men about the completion of work between groups. If men are not returning their homework, facilitators should attempt to problem-solve the situation in a non-shaming manner. Common barriers to homework completion include issues related to time management, literacy, and comprehension. These issues should be addressed one-on-one with men and specific suggestions or resources should be provided. Men's response to these interventions can be documented in the final report.*

Session 3: Developing Discrepancy
Helping Men Make The Choice To Do Things Differently

Goal: To develop sufficient trust and motivation to engage men in the process of examining their fathering

Exercises and Handouts	Content of Exercise
Check-in (10 min)	Do a brief check-in with men with the question: "How are you feeling tonight?" Complete genograms for men who were absent last session.
Exercise 1: Review of Homework (40 min)	For homework last week, men were asked to identify hopes that they have for their relationships with their children. Facilitators should ask men to share at least one of their hopes with the group in the form of a goal. Facilitators may ask the group to give feedback.
Exercise 2: Decision Point (50 min)	
Option 1. Continued Discussion of Family Expeirences and Patterns	The aim of this session is to build motivation. Last session, men began to discuss experiences of their fathers that they did and did not want to repeat. If the last session went well, facilitators can continue the discussion this week.
Option 2. Developing Discrepancy With Fathering Circles	Have men complete fathering circles. Men are asked to indicate the proportion of the circle devoted to specific feelings (e.g., anger, pride) and to compare current and desired feelings around the father-child relationship.
Option 3. Facing the Wall	Reflect that men often feel as though they are facing a wall. Discuss how men's tendency to fight against or attack the wall often leads to stronger walls. Discuss strategies that may help men make the wall smaller.
Homework (10 min)	Instruct men to complete the "Fathering log", which asks them to track their healthy and unhealthy fathering behaviors.

Session 3: Developing Discrepancy
Helping Men Make The Choice To Do Things Differently

Goal: To develop sufficient trust and motivation to engage men in the process of examining their fathering

Theme: This session continues to develop discrepancies between men's current fathering and healthier ways of relating to their children. We begin by having men check in with their hopes and goals. Men then participate in one of three exercises that aim to draw links between their current behaviors as fathers and their hopes for being better fathers. These exercises facilitate the development of men's engagement in group and motivation to change.

Materials Required for Session 3

- Worksheet: Feelings Sheet

- Worksheets: Fathering Circles Past, Present and Ideal for Option 2

Check-in (10 min)

Facilitators should invite men to check in briefly with a word that describes their current feelings. Men can be referred to the Feelings Sheet in their workbook for a list of possible feelings. Challenge men to come up with a genuine feeling, rather than a descriptor such as "fine", "OK", or "good."

> **PROCESS NOTES:**
>
> *Prior to beginning check-in, facilitators need to discuss whether they will or will not check in with the group. Because check-ins often serve a supportive function for men, we recommend that facilitators do not check in. This way, facilitators clearly maintain their role as therapists, rather than as peers or participants.*

Avoid Getting Stuck on Men's Anger

Facilitators may feel inclined to start this session by having men reflect on their thoughts about the last group, or their thoughts over the week. Because it is still early in the process, there is a relatively high potential for men to become stuck on unresolved issues about the nature or conditions of their referral. Next week, facilitators will return to the issue of impressions of group, when men have a better sense of the types of exercises and activities that will be pursued. Therefore, if possible, it is best to delay longer and more in-depth check-ins until next session.

Exercise 1: Review of Homework: Hopes I Have for my Relationship With my Child (40 min)

Have each man share one of the hopes that he has for his relationships with his children. As part of this discussion, help men to translate this hope into a goal for their involvement in *Caring Dads*. For example, if a man states that his hope is to have his children listen better, a facilitator may gently direct him to consider the goal of learning about when children listen best and to develop better skills for communicating with his children.

PROCESS NOTES:

As men talk about their hopes, it is important to focus them on behaviors over which they have control, while at the same time maintaining a supportive, accepting, and non-confrontational stance. For example, if a man reports that his motivation to attend group is to make his child protection worker happy, this response should be accepted. At the same time, this may be an opportunity to help shape men's thinking by directing them to consider how their behavior affects their circumstances. In this case the man may be asked how his group attendance may make his child protection worker happy, and why this is an important goal for a healthier relationship with his children.

This activity may also provide an opportunity to build group cohesion by having the group give feedback on each man's goal. Explain to the group that part of its purpose will be to help each man reach his goals. So, in agreeing to support a man's goal, the group is agreeing also to help in this process.

Exercise 2: Decision Point (50 min)

At this point, the goal of the *Caring Dads* sessions is to empathize with men, engage them, and enhance their motivation for change. With this in mind, facilitators should make a choice about which of the following activities will be best suited to the group. Three activity options are provided. If facilitators found that last session's discussion of the things that fathers wanted to do the same as and differently than their fathers was going well but was incomplete, they can return to this discussion (Option 1).

If it does not seem that sufficient discrepancy was developed last session to motivate men to examine their own behavior as fathers, or if this discussion was not very helpful, facilitators may choose the Fathering Circles: Past, Present and Ideal exercise (Option 2).

If facilitators sense that a main issue for this group is men's anger with their situations and feel that many men seem to be "stuck" in this anger facilitators may wish to use the Facing the Wall exercise (Option 3).

Option 1: Continue discussion of men's experience with thier fathers and desire for change

Last session, men began to brainstorm a list of things that they wanted to do the same as their fathers and things that they wanted to do differently than their fathers. Review the lists generated last session and ask men if they have further thoughts about these lists. Continue a discussion with men about their motivation to do things differently than their fathers. When possible, use men's genograms to help them see repeating cycles of maladaptive parenting and to build their motivation to change this pattern with their own children.

Facilitators who choose this exercise option should review process notes from last session. They should also consider the process notes, cautions and considerations for men who have abused their children's mothers that are listed in Option 2.

Option 2: Fathering circles: Past, present and ideal

Part 1: Ask men to brainstorm a list of feelings they had towards their fathers when they were children. Some of the feelings that are typically mentioned include: respect, love, fear, intimidation, confusion, shame, pride, rejection, hurt, loyalty, security, safety, anger, hopelessness, betrayal, powerlessness.

Have men turn to the "My Father" exercise (Fathering Circle Past) in their books and fill out the circles to reflect the feelings that they had towards their fathers when they were children. Men should use "pie pieces" to represent the amount of each feeling that they had. For example, if men felt mostly confused about their father, a large section of the circle should be devoted to the feeling of confusion.

Encourage men to share the composition of their circle with the group. For effective time management, facilitators may have men share the two or three biggest sections on their wheels rather than their entire circle.

Part 2: Have men turn to the "How I Think My Child Feels" exercise (Fathering Circle Present) in their handbook. This worksheet has men consider how their own children feel about them. Emphasize to men that it takes a lot of work and communication to know how another person feels, so we are asking them to report on how they think their child feels - this may or may not reflect the actual feelings of men's children.

Have men share their responses with the group and reflect on patterns of similarity and differences in their past and current relationships. Help men focus on their intention to behave in ways that will shift their children's feelings towards them.

Part 3: Time permitting, it may make sense to proceed to the exercise "How I Want My Child to Feel" (Fathering Circle Ideal). In this exercise men complete circles to represent how they wish their children would feel toward them.

Facilitators should draw the links between this exercise and the goals that men listed at the beginning of the session. Make the point that often, the most important starting point in changing a relationship is considering and addressing feelings. Emphasize that men need to begin to consider how each of their actions fits into these pie charts and helps, or hurts, their goal of having a better relationship with their child. For example, if a man's goal is to have his child listen to him, ask him to reflect on the feelings that children would need to have towards him to promote good listening.

What Does "Respect" Mean?

When men mention respect as a feeling that they had towards their fathers, it is important to deconstruct this word. Often, men mean that they feared their father, or feared doing something wrong. Explain that people use "respect" to mean a variety of different things, and that we can think about gaining respect in different ways. Two main ways respect is gained are through fear and through esteem. Explain that the true meaning of respect is the latter, "consideration and value for another person or thing." From then on, encourage clarity whenever men mention respect. Have them differentiate whether they are referring to fear-based, forced respect or to earned, love-based respect.

During a discussion of respect, men may challenge facilitators with statements such as: "I think it is good for kids to have some fear of their fathers." Facilitators may ask men to consider their current close friendships and intimate relationships, and reflect on whether fear is a desirable part of these relationships. Make the point that all people (including their children) are much less likely to reveal their thoughts and feelings to someone whom they fear, and that we want to encourage our children to share their feelings to help develop a closer relationship with them.

Men Whose Main Issue is Abuse of Their Children's Mother

To benefit clients referred primarily for abuse of their children's mothers, facilitators should look for opportunities to make connections between men's roles as fathers and their roles as partners. For example, during this exercise, facilitators can ask a man to describe how his father treated his mother, and to consider how that felt to him as a child. They may then encourage men to think about how their treatment of their children's mother affects their children and the father-child relationship.

Option 3: Facing the wall

In some groups, a majority of men present with feelings of extreme anger towards "the system." These men often feel as though they are caught in a helpless situation in which others perceive them as guilty until proven innocent. If anger is a major barrier to change for a majority of men in the group, working through the analogy of a wall or obstacle is sometimes helpful in encouraging clients to consider how their behaviors have an impact on their situation.

Draw a picture of a brick wall on the board and reflect that men feel as though they are constantly coming up against this brick wall.

Engage men in a brainstorm of the types of feelings that they have in facing this brick wall (e.g., anger, hopelessness, disillusionment, shame).

Point out that, in response to these feelings, men often behave in ways that have them "running into the wall", and "trying to smash the wall down." For example, men may have yelled at a child protection worker, involved their partner in lengthy court proceedings, or repeatedly argued with their partner about methods of parenting.

Suggest that other people have been responding to these attempts by strengthening the wall. Facilitators can illustrate this by drawing another row of bricks on the wall. Make the point that each time a man tries to "attack" the wall, they are likely to prompt others to strengthen it. This cycle results in men feeling more trapped.

Assert that men's strategies to smash the wall down are unsuccessful and that men need to find ways of removing the wall instead of running into it. This analogy is helpful because it also allows counsellors to make the point that change is likely to take a long time for men in this situation, especially if the wall is now many layers thick.

> ### PROCESS NOTES FOR OPTION 3:
>
> *It is important that facilitators do not let this exercise degenerate into men colluding with each other in their complaints about the various systems with which they are involved. If this shift occurs, facilitators should direct men to consider whether their negative comments are likely to strengthen the wall or break down the wall.*
>
> *Occasionally a man may assert that a wall is the best thing to have between himself and the system or himself and his partner. Ask him to reflect on whether that wall is helpful for his children as well.*

Homework (10 min)

For homework this week, men will begin to keep a diary of their parenting behavior. As part of this diary, men are asked to make a record of things they felt good about as a father, ways that they praised their children, and aspects of fathering that were more challenging. This diary is assigned to help men attend more to both their own behavior and to their children during the week, to help facilitators keep track of men's progress, and to increase the extent to which men praise their children.

Some men will report being unable to complete this homework because they see their child or children only every other weekend. Facilitators should challenge men to think broadly about their role as a father. For example, if men have access to their children in person every other week, they can praise them over the telephone. If men have no contact with their children, they can still consider the positive and challenging aspects of being a father over the week (e.g., "I felt good about respecting my restraining order, but I struggled with missing my children").

GOAL 2:

To increase men's awareness of child-centered fathering

General Notes

Goal 2: To increase men's awareness of child-centered fathering

The second goal of *Caring Dads* focuses on *increasing men's awareness of child-centered fathering*. In sessions 4 to 9, men will be educated and challenged to think about what children need to be healthy and happy. Men who are abusive require opportunities to explicitly think and talk about children's needs for a number of reasons. First, research has shown that parents who maltreat their children may have unrealistic expectations for their children and show little insight into what children really need. For example, they may expect a six year-old to take on household chores that would be more appropriate for a 10 year-old, and subsequently feel angry when the child fails to meet these expectations. Second, child behaviors that may be normal and age appropriate are often perceived as intentionally hostile or antagonistic. For example, a father may feel that his two-year old is tantrumming to cause his father embarrassment in a public place, rather than realizing that tantrums are normal for children this age. Given this unrealistic thinking, an important goal of intervention is to increase fathers' understanding of their children. Fathers may also have attitudes that run counter to children's needs such as the belief that boys over the age of 6 are "sissified" by physical affection from their fathers.

There are four components that are integral to the second goal. In order to engage in child-centered parenting, fathers need an understanding of the stages of child development, they need to understand their own child(ren) better, they need to appreciate their children's relationships with their mothers and they need to understand that parenting involves identifying and balancing the needs of children and adults. Within this balancing of needs, fathers must also be challenged to evaluate issues of power and control more realistically, and to begin taking responsibility for the power they have in the parent-child relationship.

Key therapeutic skills for this section include:

1. Modeling hopefulness

Once men have lowered their defensiveness somewhat and begin to take an open look at the relationships they have with their children, they may be overwhelmed by the enormity of the changes required to foster more positive relationships in their family. It is important for facilitators to convey a sense of hopefulness. This stance requires an attitude that simultaneously recognizes the difficulty of changing long-held patterns of thinking and behaving, but also recognizes that change is possible. Facilitators should be vigilant to even small examples of ways that men are thinking or behaving differently. Noting areas of change will help convey a sense of hopefulness to the whole group.

2. Modeling positive communication

Facilitators have a unique opportunity to model respectful and open communication behaviors for fathers. The communication between male and female co-facilitators will convey important messages about gender equity. For some of the clients, this model may be one of the few healthy male-female relationships they have observed. Facilitators should be cautious about the use of sarcasm and humor with each other, particularly at the beginning of the intervention. One of the important lessons will be for men to experience another adult (i.e., a facilitator) disagreeing with their opinion or challenging them, but doing it in a way that is respectful of them and all members of the group. Facilitators should attempt to monitor both their verbal and nonverbal behavior during sessions. It is often helpful to record sessions on videotape and to review them later with specific attention to the communication between co-facilitators.

3. Delivering information in a way that your audience can hear it

Much of the work in the second goal involves teaching men about children. Although much of this information may seem straightforward to facilitators, men may not believe or may actively reject the information being presented. The concept of cognitive authority is an important piece for understanding the processes at work. Simply put, we all make judgments about how credible or expert a source is, and pay attention to information from that source accordingly. Facilitators should be aware that having professional credentials and experience does not necessarily grant them cognitive authority with the men in the group. Many members of the public are skeptical of the idea that parenting can be researched or taught, and may be very dismissive of parenting "experts" who are young or do not have children. Establishing cognitive authority with the group will require relationship building, being genuine, admitting when a situation is difficult, and having patience. It will also be helpful to present information in a way that attempts to incorporate some of men's experiences and world views.

4. Developing parenting skills

Men in the *Caring Dads* groups often show limited effectiveness in basic parenting skills such as praising children, or being a good listener. These behaviors are taught explicitly in the program. To effectively teach a skill, facilitators need to break the skill into small steps, demonstrate effective use of the skill, and provide men with the opportunity to practice the skill and receive feedback. Ultimately, the goal is to raise men's self-efficacy with relation to these skills. Self-efficacy incorporates two components – first, that men can do the behavior effectively, and second, that men believe they can do the behavior effectively and that it will lead to a positive outcome. Four types of experiences are known to raise self-efficacy for particular behaviors:

    a) The opportunity to see others complete the skill successfully

    b) The opportunity to complete the skill successfully

    c) The provision of immediate and inaccurate feedback

    d) The provision of these opportunities in a way that is not so anxiety-provoking as to be aversive

Facilitators should be mindful of these principles when teaching specific skills.

5. Begining to challenge fathers gently by identifying discrepancies

Although the bulk of the challenging and confrontation in Caring Dads is conducted in relation to the third program goal, there are a number of more gentle challenges that are encouraged at this point. First, facilitators can continue to point out areas of discrepancy between fathers' actual and perceived relationships with their children. For example, many fathers who claim to know their children really well are able to complete only minimal information on the "How Well do I Know My Child" quiz. Drawing attention to this discrepancy provides an indirect challenge to men in terms of how well they actually know their children. Facilitators should also be on the look-out for opportunities to have men challenge each other. For example, a man who claims that having a father show affection and nurturance to his son is detrimental could be challenged by another man who had a warmer relationship with his own father and who acknowledges the benefit of fathers nurturing their children.

6. Setting the stage for the cognitive behavioral triad

The cognitive behavioral triad is introduced during this section of Caring Dads. This triad provides a framework for men to begin to develop an awareness of how perceptions of an event shape both emotional reaction and behavioral response to that event. For example, our understanding of someone's intention will have an impact on the way we *feel* about the event and what we *do* in response to the event (men will initially have difficulty distinguishing between thoughts, feelings, and actions, so it is imperative that facilitators have a good grasp of the concepts). This foundation is critical because in the next section of Caring Dads men will be challenged to analyze situations where they acted in abusive or neglectful ways by breaking down the situation into thoughts, feelings and actions. If facilitators do not have previous experience with CBT-based interventions, they may want to do some separate reading about these concepts.

Session 4: Child-Centered Fathering

Goal: To increase men's awareness of child-centered fathering

Exercises and Handouts	Content of Exercise
Check-in (40 min)	Have men check in with a report on one important thing related to their fathering that has happened for them over the past week.
Exercise 1: Continuum of Parenting Behavior (30 min)	Explain the concept of a continuum. Put abuse at one end of the continuum and ask men: "What is at the other end?" Have men brainstorm a list of healthy behaviors and then label this end of the continuum "child-centered" behaviors.
Exercise 2: Responsive and Unresponsive Praise (30 min)	Following from this general discussion of child-centered fathering practices, facilitators should transition to a discussion of praise. Part 1: Have men brainstorm a definition of praise. Engage men in developing a list of specific things they could say to their children to provide responsive praise. Part 2: Have group co-facilitators model sarcastic, unresponsive praise. Have men distinguish this non-praise from responsive praise and provide examples. Have men reflect on why parents may use these types of "non-praise." Return to original examples and ensure that all are "responsive" praise.
Homework Assignment (10 min)	Men continue their fathering log with particular attention to their use of praise.

Session 4: Child-Centered Fathering

Goal: To increase men's awareness of child-centered fathering

Theme: This week's activities have two purposes. First, facilitators have a prolonged check-in during which men are asked to discuss an important event from the previous week. This check-in gives facilitators a chance to become more aware of the challenges that men are currently facing. Second, men are introduced to the concept of "child-centered" or nurturing fathering and discuss responsive praise as an example. These steps toward recognizing child-centered parenting are important as they provide men with a powerful relationship-building skill at an early point in the program.

Materials Required for Session 4

- Worksheet: Parenting continuum diagram

- Worksheet: Nurturing wheel

- Worksheet: When Praise is not Really Praise at all

Check-in (40 min)

Invite men to check in with a description of something significant related to their fathering that has happened in the past week (or two, if necessary). Time is built in to this exercise to allow facilitators to ask each man detailed questions about their situation.

> ### PROCESS NOTES:
>
> *Long check-ins, such as this one, provide an opportunity for facilitators to demonstrate respect for each man's unique situation, to monitor men's progress, and to encourage group members to support each other as they share their personal situations in more detail. Later in the group, longer check-ins also provide the opportunity for facilitators to challenge men to use more positive and less harmful parenting strategies.*
>
> *To ensure that Caring Dads maintains its focus on intervention rather than support, facilitators should monitor the amount of time spent in check-ins. If facilitators observe that check-ins are consistently extending beyond the designated time limit, they may decide to limit check-in time. This can be done by informing each man of the time limit he has to check in (e.g., each man may have 5 minutes) and assigning one group member as a timekeeper. Facilitators may also want to talk individually with men who are having difficulty staying within reasonable check-in time frames.*

Exercise 1: Continuum of Parenting Behavior (30 min)

Begin this exercise by drawing a line on the flip chart with two ends, and identifying this line as a continuum. Explain to men that a continuum refers to two extremes of the same type of behaviors. Some behaviors fall at one end while other behaviors may fall somewhere between both ends.

Label one end of the continuum "parent-centered/abusive behaviors." The facilitator may wish to mention that although the group will eventually discuss parent-centered/abusive behaviors, the initial focus is on the opposite end of the continuum (child-centered behaviors).

Have men consider what behaviors might be at the positive end of the continuum. Write men's responses in the appropriate position on the continuum. Behaviors that often come up in this brainstorm include:

- Showing love and attention (e.g., hugs, kisses, "I love you")
- Trying to be understanding
- Having fair and reasonable limits
- Giving kids their space
- Recognizing children's rights
- Being there for children to talk to
- Being respectful of children's mothers
- Being consistent
- Being interested in, and part of, children's worlds (e.g., their music)

Label this end of the continuum child-centered behaviors because behaviors listed at this end are focused on the needs of the child. Ask men to brainstorm how children who experience these child-centered behaviors may feel. Men may respond by saying that children feel loved, understood, respected, and appreciated.

Continuum of Parenting Behaviors

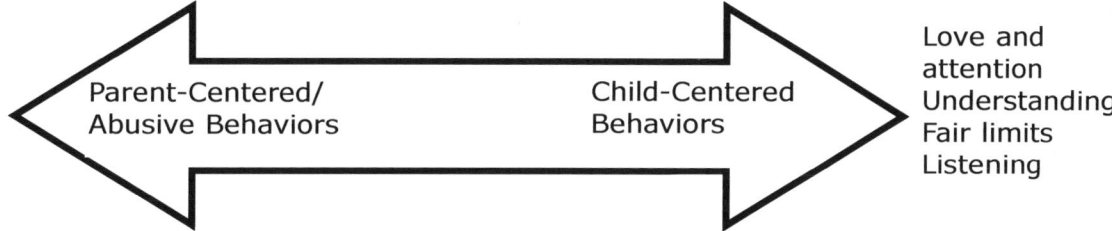

Refer men to the the Nurturing Wheel provided in their workbooks as a review of these positive parenting behaviors. To end this exercise, ask men to reflect on whether fathers or children have the power to decide what end of the spectrum parenting falls on. Facilitators should identify that parents have more power than children. Children have no recourse - there is virtually nothing they can do if they do not like how their parents are acting. Children also don't know any better - they assume that whatever is happening in their family is normal. Children have no economic resources, they are seldom physically stronger than their parents, and they don't have the same experience or understanding of the world. In all these ways, parents, rather than children, are the ones who have the power to decide where their parenting will fall on the continuum.

In My Family, the Children Have All the Power

Sometimes men will challenge the notion of children being powerless by raising the point that children have been taught to call Child Protection Services or complain to teachers and other authorities if they do not like the way they are being parented. If this occurs, re-direct the discussion to basic issues of who gets to make important decisions, economic resources, cognitive ability, etc. Empahsize that even if children do complain to others, they cannot do anything else and ultimately, it is those others who may then have power.

Be Sure to Include Support of Children's Mothers

Ensure some of the behaviors listed on the child-centered end of the continuum involve working collaboratively and supportively with children's mothers, (e.g., "working together with my child's mother"). Men seldom generate these types of examples spontaneously, but will if facilitators ask questions about what might be needed in the child's family for there to be child-centered parenting.

Exercise 2: Responsive and Unresponsive Praise (30 min)

Part 1: Responsive Praise

Ask men to define the word "praise." We look for a definition that is something like "saying something with approval or admiration that makes someone feel good about themselves."

Ask men to think about the most meaningful praise that they received as a child. Have men share examples of this praise with each other.

Explain that the most effective praise is praise that is direct, specific, related to the child's immediate behavior and linked to something about which the child feels proud. For example, "you did an excellent job of working quietly at your homework tonight" is much more effective than the statement "you were really good tonight." Specific statements of praise allow the child to know what they are being praised for, which encourages them to repeat this behavior.

Part 2: Unresponsive Praise

Have men turn to the handout in their book called: "When praise is not really praise at all" and read through the examples. This handout outlines that praise is not really praise when it is qualified, sarcastic, dishonest, etc. Facilitators should role play the various forms of ineffective praise and have men identify what is being role played by finding the description on the hand-out. For example, one facilitator can role play ineffective praise of a child's grades in school, by telling the child (played by the other facilitator) that:

- Look at that! Your grades are almost as good as your brother's.

- How did I manage to produce a child who is such a geek?

- (sarcastically) Well, these grades are really stellar - I can't believe that the teacher even gives out grades this high.

- This looks pretty good, but it is too bad that you can't seem to do any better in math.

- Look at those grades! You are certainly taking after me, and not your mother. When I was in grade 4, I got perfect marks almost all the time. It looks like you are doing almost as well, which is pretty good given your mother's genes."

Have men reflect on how this unresponsive praise might affect a child. How might a child feel hearing these things?

Return to the list generated in Part 1 of this exercise, and ensure that all of the examples provided were examples of responsive praise.

Overall, Part 2 of this exercise is meant to be brief. Facilitators mainly want to ensure that the praise that men are providing to their children is genuine.

Note that there is a lot to cover in this exercise. Remember that the point of this session is to encourage men to build capacity with the skill of praising their children. If there is not time to complete both parts of the praise exercise, do only Part 1 in group. Ask men to review the handout at home. Then, during check-in next week, review the key concepts about praise that really isn't praise. Practice evaluating whether statements are genuine praise using the examples men provide during check-in.

> **PROCESS NOTES:**
>
> *It has been our experience that men are relatively poor at generating examples of praise from their own experiences with their children. Thus, in this initial exercise, it is helpful for facilitators to provide men with hypothetical examples where the praise that might be provided is fairly obvious.*

Praise and Non-Praise of Children's Mothers

Facilitators might want to point out that fathers also provide praise and "non-praise" to the mothers of their children both in what they say to her and in what they say to their children about her (e.g., "Look at that! Your mother was actually organized enough to send everything she needed for you. What a surprise"). If the majority of the group consists of men with a history of domestic violence, facilitators may consider using father-mother examples of responsive and unresponsive praise for parenting, in addition to father-child examples. The homework exercise can also be adapted around what men may say to their children about their mother.

This is one of the first opportunities that facilitators have to address some of men's negative attitudes and behaviors towards their children's mothers. It is critical that facilitators set a norm, at this early stage, that hostile attitudes and behaviors directed at children' mothers are also important to consider. If facilitators fail to assert this position early on, and instead support men in their negative attitudes, it will become more and more difficult to challenge men about their hostility and abuse of children's mothers as the program proceeds.

Homework (10 min)

For homework this week, men are asked to continue to keep their diary of parenting behavior. Ask men to pay particular attention to the section of their parenting log that asks them to record three ways that they have praised their children.

Session 5: Building Relationships With Our Children

Goal: To increase men's awareness of child-centered fathering

Exercises and Handouts	Content of Exercise
Check-in and Homework Review (40 min)	Have men check in with an example from their homework of a way that they praised their children over the past week. Write men's examples of praise on the flip-chart. Direct men to examine the impact of their praise on their children and how it felt to praise their child. Reinforce appropriate use of praise.
Exercise 1: Decision Point (50 min) Option 1: How Well do I Know my Child?	Provide men with 10 to 15 minutes to complete the "How well do I know my child" quiz in their books. Have men reflect on how much they know their child and on which questions were most difficult to answer.
Option 2: My Child's Identifications	Have men brainstorm a list of groups with which their children identify (e.g., cultural groups). How do men support their children's varied identities?
Homework Assignment (20 min)	In addition to keeping their fathering log, men are asked to complete questions from the "How well do I know my child" quiz that they were unable to complete in group. Extra quiz forms are included for men who have more than one child.

Session 5: Building Relationships With Our Children

Goal: To increase men's awareness of child-centered fathering

Theme: At the beginning of this session, facilitators continue a discussion of men's praise of their children by having them present and discuss concrete examples of praise they used in the past week. Solidifying understanding of appropriate praise is important, because increasing men's use of positive reinforcement and praise is an excellent way to quickly improve men's relationships with their children, and hopefully begin to move toward more positive cycles of parent-child interaction. During the second part of this session, facilitators address another issue critical to improving the father-child relationship - men's attention to, and knowledge of, their children. Men are prompted to evaluate how well they know and understand their children. Advantages of knowing children are emphasized, and potential dangers of lacking knowledge are reviewed. This exercise also challenges a perception of children as property or extensions of their families or fathers.

Materials Required for Session 5

- Worksheet: "How Well Do I Know My Child" quiz for different age groups

Check-in and Homework Review (40 min)

Facilitators should invite men to check in with a specific example of how they praised their children in the past week. Write men's examples on the flip-chart for reference. Facilitators should direct men to examine the impact of their praise on their child or children. It may also be useful to ask men how it felt to praise their child - was it something that took more effort or attention than they predicted? What was most difficult about avoiding the ineffective praise traps?

> **PROCESS NOTES:**
>
> *If facilitators did not have time last week to finish the exercise on responsive and unresponsive praise, they can complete it at this time (see notes from previous section).*
>
> *Facilitators should provide ample reinforcement for men's examples of genuine praise, even if they are not stellar examples. This positive reinforcement will help develop men's self-efficacy and their perception of the group as a safe environment for sharing personal examples.*

Beware of Extended Check-ins

Facilitators should note that it is very easy to fall into patterns of extending check-in periods and using the time to provide individual counselling to a few of the more outspoken men in the group. Facilitators need to work together to monitor the amount of time that they spend with each man during these check-in periods and to ensure equity in support provided. Alternatively, facilitators can have each man specify the amount of time he needs from the group and can track men's time. Facilitators who find that they are spending a good deal of time helping men solve child management crises during check-in may want to review sessions 15 and 16 for suggestions on how to best manage men's concerns.

Praising Children's Mothers

Men who are primarily referred for issues relating to their partner may assert that they have no difficulties praising their children and may "toss off" examples. In this case, challenge men to pick a more difficult task - praising children's mothers. The praise may not be provided directly to mothers if men have no ongoing contact, but may be something fathers have said to their children that also supports the mother-child relationship (e.g., "You and your mother are both really good at knowing the right thing to say at the right time".)

Exercise 1: Decision Point (50 min)

This session, facilitators will work with men to have them evaluate how well they know their children. If facilitators feel that most men in the group have limited knowledge of their children, they may wish to use the "How well do I know my child" quiz to help men be more reflective (Option 1). If fathers have a reasonable amount of knowledge of their children, but need to develop greater empathy for their children, Option 2 may be a better choice.

Option 1: How well do I know my child?

Facilitators should direct men to the "How well do I know my child" quiz. Note that slightly different versions of this quiz are provided for children of different ages. Provide 10 to 15 minutes for men to complete this quiz. If there is a need for greater group cohesion, facilitators may have men interview each other for the answers to these questions, rather than complete them individually.

After men have completed this quiz, ask each man to reflect on the completeness of their knowledge of their child. Men generally have more difficulties with questions about children's feelings (i.e., worries, hopes) than their likes or activities. Ask men to reflect on why they might have more difficulties with these questions.

Facilitators may also ask men why they think this exercise was assigned. This discussion provides an opportunity to review the parenting continuum from last week and the idea that to become a more child-centered parent, it is necessary to know and understand children and their experiences. Because of the power imbalance in adult-child relationships, there is less pressure to know and understand your children than there is to know and understand others in your life (e.g., partner, boss, co-workers). By the end of this discussion, facilitators should have presented the following points:

- If adults do not know their children, they are more likely to ignore or be unable to identify their children's reactions to what adults do.

- If adults do not know their children, they are more likely to ignore their children's needs, hopes, and wishes. Children are independent, autonomous beings who deserve to have their fathers respect their wishes and needs.

- Children naturally wish for involvement, acceptance, and love from their fathers. Because children seek these things, it is almost never too late to start attending more to their needs, wishes, and interests.

Facilitators may conclude this exercise with a discussion of how fathers might get to know their children better. Examples of positive ways that men can get to know their children better include listening to children, watching their activities, and encouraging them to have friends over. Be sure to review and label intrusive and harmful ways to invade children's privacy. Examples of intrusive methods are going through their rooms, reading their diaries, or listening in on their phone conversations. If men are resistant to the harm of these methods (i.e., "I have a right to know what my child is doing, even if it means reading her diary"), have them reflect on whether they would be more or less inclined to confide in, or talk to, someone who had invaded their privacy in this way.

> **PROCESS NOTES:**
>
> *Facilitators need to be aware of literacy issues for this exercise. It may be necessary to pair up a facilitator and a man who has difficulty reading these questions or responding in a written format.*
>
> *Opportunities may again come up during this exercise to make intergenerational links between men's experiences with their own fathers to the experiences of their children. For example, a man who is committed to not abandoning his children (like his father did) still may have very little knowledge of the interests or personalities of his children.*
>
> *An appropriate theme that often arises is the need for men to have greater patience with their children, and for men to stop, watch, and think about their children and what they might be thinking and feeling. This insight shows that men are progressing appropriately for this stage of the group.*
>
> *Another theme that may come up is differences in men's experiences with their different children. Facilitators can use this opportunity to point out that although men may feel that they have more in common with one of their children, each of their children has unique needs, desires, and wishes that their father should respect.*

Option 2: My child's identifications

Faciltiators should start by explaining that part of what makes each of us unique is our sense of self, our sense of "who we are". Part of this sense of self comes from our identifications with groups. For example, people identify with different gender, age, cultural, and community groups. Like adults, children's sense of self is also partially determined by their identifications.

Ask men to brainstorm a list of their own identifications. Included in this list should be differences in culture, religion and language, as well as possibly differences based on men's socioeconomic status, employment or living situations.

Work with men to brainstorm a similar list of identifications for each of their children. Remind men to think back to other identifications that are common for children and teens. For example, teenagers may identify as "druggies" or "geeks", and as "freshmen" or "seniors".

Ask men to speculate on why it is important to understand their children's identifications. Make the point that nurturing children's developing sense of self requires understanding of children's identifications.

Children as Property of Their Parents

Facilitators should be alert to indications that men see their children as property or extensions of themselves. These attitudes may be conveyed through men's indifference to their children's emotional lives or men's tendency to identify what their child "should" want, need or identify with. Facilitators should prompt men to view their children as independent, autonomous people. Viewing children as autonomous is essential if men are going to develop greater understanding of, and empathy for, their children. In addition, such a view frees men to evaluate their children's misbehavior as the unique experiences or reactions of a developing person, rather than as solely reflections of their success or failure as a parent.

Including children's mothers

The "How well do I know my child" quiz includes questions specifically addressing children's relationships with their mothers. For example, men are asked what their children like to do best with their mother and what they worry about in regard to their mothers. Facilitators can highlight these questions with men in the group who have an abusive or conflictual relationship with their children's mother. Mothers may also be brought into the identification option, by having men reflect on how their child's identity has also been shaped by their mothers. In both cases, make the point that to know and understand their children, fathers also need to appreciate and understand other important relationships in their children's lives, particularly their children's relationships to their mothers.

Extra Time Option

Sometimes men will present with seeming unconcern about their lack of knowledge of their children. One way to address this is to return to a discussion of men's history. Ask men to think of situations in their families where they were badly treated and reflect on what may have been different if their father knew and understood them. Have men complete the sentence "I wish my father had known that..." Depending on where men are in processing their own experiences, this reflecting can be a powerful exercise and may help men to fully appreciate the importance of better knowledge of their children.

Homework (20 min)

For homework this week, men continue to keep their diary of parenting behavior. In addition, men may be asked to find out the answers to questions that they didn't know on the "How well do you know your child quiz?" and/or completing this quiz or the identification exercise with respect to their other children.

Session 6: Listening To Children

Goal: To increase men's awareness of child-centered fathering

Exercises and Handouts	Content of Exercise
Check-in and Thoughts on Homework (30 min)	Men should check in with a review of issues that might have arisen in the past week. Facilitators should look for opportunities to invite men to talk about thoughts they had about the homework assignment. As appropriate, challenge men to continue to take the time necessary to know their children better.
Exercise 1: Listening to Children (20 min)	Introduce the concept of good listening behavior using role play. Generate a list of characteristics of good and poor listening.
Exercise 2: Tips for Being a Good Listener (20 min)	Ask men to reflect on their own style of listening and consider barriers to better listening. Review the "Tips For Being a Good Listener" worksheet.
Exercise 3: Relationship Building Challenges (30 min)	This exercise functions as a review of material covered over the past few sessions. Ask men to complete the "Relationship building challenges" worksheet. Engage men in considering ways to address these barriers to develop better relationships with their children.
Homework Assignment (10 min)	Men are challenged to identify specific ways to reduce barriers to building better relationships with their children.

Session 6: Listening To Children

Goal: To increase men's awareness of child-centered fathering

Theme: This week continues to focus on fathers' positive behavior. After men have reflected on their week (and on the homework quiz), facilitators help men explore good and poor listening. An in-group modeling experience helps men to recognize the importance of this skill. Men are also given explicit guidelines for listening to their children. After this introduction, men complete an exercise on relationship building challenges. This exercise functions as a review of the child-centered fathering behaviors covered over the last three weeks. It also represents a transition to more challenging and personalized material, as men are asked to reflect on and challenge personal barriers to building healthier relationships with their children.

Materials Required for Session 6

- Worksheet: Tips For Being a Good Listener

- Worksheet: Relationship Building Challenges

Check-in and Thoughts on Homework (30 min)

Ask men to check in with a review of significant parenting events over the past week. Look for opportunities to invite men to comment on their thoughts about this homework assignment. Because the "How well do I know my child?" exercise is powerful for many men, facilitators should be ready to discuss issues that may have been triggered by this exercise.

> **PROCESS NOTES:**
>
> *For some fathers, the time spent with their children to fill out this quiz may be one of the longest continuous periods of time that they have spent focusing on their children's needs. If this seems to be the case, facilitators should point it out and encourage fathers to spend more time attending to their children. Facilitators may observe that when men are not spending this time with their children, they are slipping towards parent-centered fathering.*
>
> *Be aware of the content of men's sharing. It may be necessary to reflect that men are limiting their discussion to factual information they have discovered about their children. If this occurs, discuss why factual information might be easier to share or notice than other aspects of children's lives, such as children's feelings. Challenge men to share a range of information and observations about their children. Reflect on the impact of knowing factual, versus emotional, information about children.*
>
> *Facilitators should also be alert to examples where men have "found out" something about their child in an inappropriate or intrusive way (e.g., finding something out through a third party). Ask the group to comment on whether learning about a child in this manner is child-centered.*

Criticism of Children's Mothers

Facilitators need to be alert for men's indirect criticism of the parenting choices made by their children's mother (e.g., I found out my child doesn't go to bed at a reasonable hour when his mother is caring for him). Stress that the goal is to come to a better understanding of the child's emotional life (likes, dislikes, fears, sources of pride), not to engage in comparisons of who is a better parent.

Exercise 1: Listening to Children (20 min)

Explain that listening to children is a core parenting skill that is crucial for building healthy parent-child relationships. Ask for a volunteer to help role play a situation in which a child wants his or her parent to listen. For example, one of the men could role play a 10 year-old coming home from school feeling rejected by peers. The facilitator, who is playing the role of the parent, should exaggerate some of the poor listening characteristics in the following lists, such as offering excessive advice, interrupting etc. After the role play, ask the group to identify poor listening behaviors.

Good Listeners	Poor Listeners
• Maintain good eye contact, as appropriate with children • Focus on the person talking • Face the person talking • Ask questions for clarification but don't "interrogate" • Avoid interrupting or arguing • Avoid providing advice before understanding the full story • Reflect the feelings of the person talking	• Do not focus on the person talking and may be distracted by other things • Ask irrelevant questions • Interrupt • Do not appear to be listening (e.g., no eye contact, body facing away) • Focus on themselves • Give advice before really understanding the problem

Debriefing should include asking the man who was role playing the child how he felt (e.g., not heard, frustrated, unvalued) and asking other men to brainstorm the feelings they experience when someone is not listening to them. This exercise can help men practice taking the perspective of their children. The scene should be replicated with good listening.

A good supplement to this exercise is to have men practice listening. Put men in pairs, and have them work together to create a role play demonstrating good listening. Facilitators can then have men present their role plays to the group.

> **PROCESS NOTES**
>
> *Having men link their experiences of being listened to (or not listened to) to their emotional reaction is an important empathy-building opportunity.*
>
> *Facilitators should draw the link between men's frustration when they are not feeling heard, and how children feel when they are not being listened to.*

Exercise 2: Tips for Being a Good Listener (20 min)

Refer men to the "Tips for Being a Good Listener" worksheet. Review the worksheet with the men, making the following points.

1. Make time for your children

Children need time to talk to their fathers. Encourage men to think about when their children are most likely to want to talk and to try to be available at that time. Suggest to men that one good time for many children is right after school or before children go to bed.

2. Pay attention

Fathers need to focus their attention on what their children are saying. This is not as easy as it sounds! Encourage men to turn off the television or computer and to try to reduce distractions. If men are not able to stop what they are doing, suggest that they consider whether it is better to ask their children if they can talk in 15 minutes when they are more able to focus on what their child is saying.

3. Resist fixing the problem

Reflect that a parent's first impulse when listening to a child's problem is often to jump in to offer advice or fix the problem. Emphasize that fathers need to resist these urges, at least until they fully understand their children's perspectives. This is especially important when children are 7 or older because, at this age, children gain a good deal of self-esteem from dealing with their problems by themselves.

4. Ask questions

If men are not offering advice or fixing the problem - what should they be doing while listening to their children? One important thing that fathers can do is to ask their children questions. Emphasize that these questions need to be specific because children have much more difficulty than adults in answering broader questions. For example, instead of asking "How did school go today?", a father can ask: "How did lunch go with David today? I know that you were worried that he wasn't going to let you sit beside him."

5. Figure out and talk about what your children are feeling

Fathers can also reflect on their children's feelings. Children benefit from having their parents figure out and try to label their feelings. For example, a father may say: "It sounds like you were really disappointed that David didn't save a seat for you at lunch."

6. Get to know how your children like to talk

Most adults prefer to talk by sitting down and facing each other. However, direct face-to-face talking is more difficult for children than it is for adults. Children may feel more comfortable talking if they don't have to make eye contact, or if they are involved in something else at the same time (e.g., drawing, shooting hoops). Fathers just need to remember that, regardless of their children's style, as fathers, their objective is to listen.

Exercise 3: Relationship Building Challenges (30 min)

Ask men to complete Part 1 of the Relationship Building Challenges exercise. In this exercise, fathers are asked to identify relationship building behaviors that they find difficult.

Facilitators should invite each man to share one of his difficulties with the group and reflect on how the impact on his child and the father-child relationship.

If there is sufficient time during the group, facilitators may wish to move to Part 2 of this exercise where men start to consider ways to reduce barriers to building better relationships with their children. Alternatively, this part of the exercise is assigned for homework.

Barriers Related to Children's Mothers

In the Relationship Building Challenges exercise, some of the items relate to men's ability to support children's relationship with their mothers. These items preview work that we return to in subsequent sessions. At this point, facilitators may need to avoid debating with men about what they can and cannot do to improve the situation with their children's mothers. Instead, encourage men to recognize that their negative attitudes towards their children's mother is impeding their relationship with their children.

Homework (10 min)

For homework this week, assign Part 2 of the Relationship Building Challenges exercise. This exercise has men identify obstacles to engaging in relationship building behaviors such as: lack of time, feelings of discomfort, worry about meeting the child's other needs, or hostile attitudes towards children's mothers. Men are asked to problem-solve for two of those difficulties in a way that does not infringe upon the rights of their child or the child's mother. Men also continue to complete their fathering log.

Session 7: Fathers As Part Of Families

Goal: To increase men's awareness of child-centered fathering

Exercises and Handouts	Content of Exercise
Check-in and Homework Review (40 min)	Have men check in with a report on one important thing that happened for them over the past week that is relevant to their fathering and/or with a review of their homework.
Exercise 1: Setting a Good Example (20 min)	Emphasize that fathers are part of families, and that how fathers feel about their families influences how their children feel. Ask men to identify people who are important in their children's lives. Ask men to brainstorm a list of behaviors that are good examples for their children in communicating with others and managing frustration. Ask men to list thoughts that connect with these behaviors.
Exercise 2: Appreciation For My Children's Mother (40 min)	Have men reflect on how well they support their children's relationship with their mother. Encourage men to speculate on the thoughts that support children's mothers. Ask men to consider how their children are affected.
Homework Assignment (10 min)	Assign men the task of being a good example to their children. They should do this by acting in a positive way towards someone important in their children's lives.

Session 7: Fathers As Part Of Families

Goal: To increase men's awareness of child-centered fathering

Theme: In the past session, facilitators introduced potential barriers to men's relationships with their children. This session builds on this foundation with a focus on men's relationships with other important people in their children's lives, particularly their children's mothers. Facilitators should emphasize that the father-child relationship does not exist independently of the child's relationships with others in their lives (e.g., mothers, grandparents, teachers). Facilitators ask men to speculate on how they are, or can be, good examples to their children in the context of their relationships with significant others. Facilitators are encouraged to help men identify thoughts and actions that support healthy and unhealthy relationships. This focus on thoughts and actions sets the stage for later learning about the cognitive behavioral triad and for change among men who are failing to support, and potentially abusing, children's mothers.

Materials Required for Session 7

- Worksheet: What kind of example do I set?

Check-in and Homework Review (40 min)

Invite men to check in with a review of their homework and/or a description of something significant that has happened recently that relates to their fathering. Ask men questions about their situations and challenge them to further eliminate barriers to developing better relationships with their children.

Exercise 2: Setting a Good Example (20 min)

For many fathers, an important barrier to building a better relationship with their children is men's relationship with other important people in their children's lives, particularly their children's mothers. Children see their fathers within the context of their relationships to their mother, and are thus affected by the marital relationship. Children are affected by how parents talk about each other, and the interactions that happen between separated parents. Children also see their fathers in interaction with the community, and learn about neighborhoods, friends, and relationships with others from the way they see their fathers act. This exercise begins to explore these relationships.

Part 1

To start this exercise, point out that men's relationships with their children are not independent of their children's other relationships. To solidify this point, ask men for examples of what they remember learning from watching their father deal with someone close to them like their mother, a grandparent, uncle, aunt, important friend or neighbor.

Part 2

Ask men to brainstorm a list of important people in their children's lives. Reinforce that children need to have many people who love and care for them. Also emphasize that conflict among the people that children care for is very difficult for children and often causes feelings of insecurity.

Part 3

Create a chart with the headings "Actions" and "Thoughts." Using the category "Communicating with Others" ask men to come up with a list of examples of how fathers could act in a way that sets a good example for their children. Once each category is finished, have men add a list of positive thoughts that would support these actions.

Men can go through the same exercise with "Managing Frustration." Ask men to generate a list of actions and thoughts that support managing their frustration and being a good example to their children.

Here is an example of the types of answers men may generate:

Actions: How could a father set a good example in communicating with others?	**Thoughts:** What thoughts support these actions?
· Being respectful of people regardless of their looks or position · Using good manners · Not swearing · Talking calmly through a problem · Not talking badly about someone behind their back	· I need to listen to this person even if I don't like what he or she is saying · Everyone deserves respect from me · No matter how others talk, I can still be polite and avoid swearing if I choose
Actions: How could a father set a good example in managing frustration?	**Thoughts:** What thoughts support these actions?
· By keeping calm, slow breathing, not getting worked up · Not losing temper, swearing or stomping off · Trying again · Not talking about it over and over again afterwards · Trying again	· I don't need to be frustrated by this · There are more important things to be worried about. I am not going to let this one get to me. · Everyone has to deal with frustrating things sometimes. · Being frustrated is not going to help me through this situation

On Frustration With Children

In doing the "Managing Frustration" part of this exercise, facilitators can acknowledge that children are sometimes frustrating. One of the jobs men have as parents is to cope with this frustration appropriately. Ask men to specifically talk about how they set an example for their children in the way they handle frustration with their children's behavior.

In this discussion it is important to help men identify as many alternative explanations as possible for frustrating child behavior. Flexible thinking about frustrating child behavior is valuable because one key risk factor for abuse is men's perception that children misbehave specifically to annoy or defy their fathers. The more explanations that men have, the more likely that they will be able to counter thoughts that their children are being frustrating with the intent to annoy or defy them.

Exercise 3: Appreciation For My Children's Mother (40 min)

Begin this exercise by having men rate themselves on the following question: "What kind of example do you set in your relationship with your children's mother?" Refer men to the handout with a rating scale from 1 to 10, where 1 is a very bad example and 10 is a very good example.

Have men share their ratings with the group. In their discussion, ask men to talk specifically about how they set a good example for their children in how they communicate, or manage frustration, with children's mothers. Be sure to follow-up on both the positive and negative behaviors. For example, if a man has rated himself as a 2, ask him first about his negative attitudes. Follow-up by asking why he rated himself as a 2 instead of a 1 – what is he doing that is at least a little bit right? Ask men to speculate on how children are affected by these positive and negative example setting behaviors.

If there is sufficient time, facilitators may repeat the actions and thoughts chart for the question: "How could a father set a good example in the way he relates to children's mothers?".

Summarize this exercise with the take home message that part of being a good father is supporting children in their relationships with others, especially their children's mothers.

Men Using Mothers as Bad Examples

Sometimes fathers will present behaviors of children's mothers as negative examples. Often when men do this, it is to provide support for their anger or disrespect for their children's mothers in the "See, I told you that that was a bad thing to do" way. Facilitators should be careful to avoid colluding with negative views of the children's mothers. One way to do so is to focus men on examples of what the fathers did. Another is to challenge men suspected of looking for ammunition in conflicts with their partner. Facilitators can use the latter as a concrete example of how men are not supporting their children's mothers, and can ask the group to reflect on the indirect effect of this action on their children.

When children's mothers have behaved in objectively negative ways (i.e., abandonment, not showing up for visits), men should still be challenged to think about how they might support their children in a way that does not disrespect the children's mothers. For example, fathers may be asked whether bad-mouthing a child's mother for not showing up for a visit in front of the child is likely to be helpful to the child. Instead, emphasize the importance of listening to the child's disappointment. Let men know that listening is critical - if they start to commiserate with children in their disappointment with their mother's behavior, they will likely make their children feel worse. Even if children are saying bad things about a parent, they do not want the other parent to say these things too.

Homework (10 min)

For homework this week, men are asked to list three things that they do that provide good examples to their children. If men are co-parenting with another parent (separated or not), challenge them to come up with one example of something that they have done for or with that parent that is a good example for their children.

Session 8: Eliminating Barriers To Better Relationships

Goal: To increase men's awareness of child-centered fathering

Exercises and Handouts	Content of Exercise
Check-in and Homework Review (40 min)	Have men check in with a report on one important thing that happened for them over the past week that is relevant to their fathering and/or with a review of their homework.
Exercise 1: Connections Between Thoughts, Feelings and Actions (30 min)	Educate men about the connections between thoughts, feelings, and actions using an example from check-in. Have men brainstorm a full list of the father's feelings. Then have men brainstorm a full list of possible thoughts. Have men speculate on the actions that this father is likely to take. Are these actions child-centered? Explain to men that, of feelings, thoughts, and actions, thoughts are the easiest to change. Have men brainstorm possible alternative thoughts for the example situation.
Exercise 2: Thoughts and Beliefs to Watch Out For (30 min)	Explain to fathers that recognizing the thoughts that are likely to lead to healthy and unhealthy behavior requires practice. Using a video clip, have men practice recognizing positive and negative thoughts.
Homework Assignment (10 min)	Men are asked to describe two times that they are irritated with their child and to list the thoughts that they are having in those times.

Session 8: Eliminating Barriers To Better Relationships

Goal: To increase men's awareness of child-centered fathering

Theme: This session, men begin to focus more closely on negative fathering behaviors. The session begins by providing men with time for a longer check-in, during which facilitators should review homework and be attentive to situations that can serve as an example to the group of the feelings, thoughts, and actions triangle. The rest of the session is devoted to exploring the connections among feelings, thoughts, and actions, and emphasizing that change occurs when men alter their thoughts. Concrete examples are provided and men are encouraged to practice identifying thoughts that are likely to lead to unhealthy fathering actions.

Materials Required for Session 8

- Worksheet: Thoughts, feelings, and actions triangle

- Worksheet: Thoughts and beliefs to watch out for

- Video clip

Check-in and Homework Review (40 min)

Invite men to check in with a review of their homework and/or a description of something significant that has happened recently that relates to their fathering. Ask men questions about their situations and challenge them to further eliminate barriers to developing better relationships with their children.

> ### PROCESS NOTES:
>
> *During check-in, facilitators should be attentive to difficult situations that can be used in the next exercise. In particular, look for:*
>
> - *A specific event where a father acted in an emotionally abusive, neglectful or otherwise unhealthy manner*
> - *A situation in which a father reports feeling that his child was "out to get him," or appears otherwise threatened by child misbehavior*
> - *A situation in which a father's interpretation lacked appropriate consideration of his child's needs or developmental limitations.*

Choosing the Right Example

In selecting an example, facilitators should be aware of the level of trust in the group. Choosing an example from a father who continues to feel very vulnerable in group and distrustful of group co-facilitators is likely to result in a high level of defensiveness and possibly, the group joining against the facilitators to support the father's defensiveness and vulnerability. If this occurs, facilitators will need to take an active and challenging role in asserting the connections among thoughts, feelings, and actions. Such actions are likely to be helpful to some men in the group, but potentially alienating to others. Therefore, it is best to select an example from a father who appears well-connected, engaged, and relatively comfortable with disclosing to the group.

Exercise 1: Connections Between Thoughts, Feelings, and Actions (30 minutes)

Explain that one step to becoming a better father is to better understand how things go wrong. Considering an example from check-in, invite one of the men in the group to give a full description of the situation. If no appropriate examples arise during check-in, facilitators may need to provide an example situation.

Have the group brainstorm a list of the father's feelings at the beginning point of this situation. Verify these feelings with the father who provided the example. Then, have the group brainstorm a list of the father's possible thoughts. Again, verify these with the father who provided the example. Ask men to evaluate or speculate on the actions that this father is likely to take. Are these actions nurturing and child-centered?

Show the triangle of feelings, thoughts, and actions and make the point that feelings, thoughts, and actions influence each other. For example, negative thoughts are likely to lead to more negative feelings. Negative behaviors are likely to generate more negative feelings and thoughts, etc. Explain to men that of feelings, thoughts, and actions, thoughts are the easiest to change.

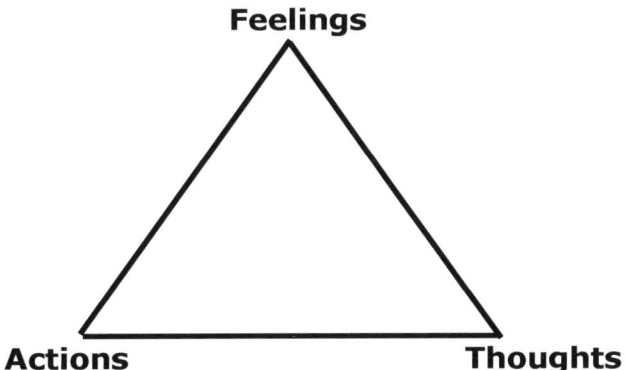

Have men brainstorm possible alternative thoughts for the example situation. Emphasize how more positive thoughts are likely to lead to both better feelings and more nurturing and child-centered actions. Inform men that future sessions will focus on alternative actions that may result from these different thoughts. An example of how this exercise is done is provided in the following box.

Situation: A father reported that he arrived home one night to find the house in a mess with toys everywhere. His 4-year-old daughter was in the middle of playing and didn't even run to greet him or give him a kiss. He walked up behind his daughter and sharply told her to put her toys away. His daughter refused in a rude manner. The father told her again, this time in a louder voice, and then walked away feeling very frustrated and annoyed that his daughter never listens to him.

Selection of a time near the beginning

A minute after the father walked in the door, just before he told his daughter to put her toys away

Brainstorm of possible feelings

Angry, annoyed, frustrated, hurt (that his daughter didn't acknowledge him), left out, ineffective, unappreciated, disrespected (that his expectation that the toys be contained is not being met)

Brainstorm of possible thoughts

Why doesn't my daughter ever listen to me
I can't believe I have to walk in on this mess
My daughter doesn't even care that I am home
What is wrong with her mother that she allows such a mess
I really shouldn't have to deal with this after a full day of work
She is the most difficult child

Evaluation of actions

Ask men: With those thoughts, what actions did the father take?
(Answer: Sharply told his daughter to clean up)

Ask men: Were these actions nurturing or child-centered?
(Answer: No, there were other ways that the father child have responded that would have been better for his daughter)

Point out that, the feelings, thoughts, and actions of this father are connected and assert that thoughts are easiest to change.

Brainstorm of alternative thoughts

My daughter must be having a lot of fun! I don't think she even heard me come in
This is going to be quite a mess to clean up, but I am sure that we will get things cleaned up before she goes to bed
My daughter is only four and her playtime is really important to her
I wonder if I can find a fun and playful way to let her know that I am home

With these thoughts, how would the fathers' actions likely change?

The father may have joined in with his daughter's games and they may have played together for a little bit
The father may have enjoyed playing with his child
The father may have been reassured that his daughter cares for him

Men often struggle with the differentiation of thoughts, feelings, and actions. For some, identifying thoughts is a very difficult task. Facilitators should emphasize that learning to identify thoughts is a skill and takes practice like anything else.

Men tend to think that behavior is the easiest angle of the triangle to change. In other words, they may believe that the best way to change is to simply decide that certain behaviors are wrong and vow not to do them anymore. Make the point that without changing the associated thoughts and feelings, the behaviors end up coming through regardless of whether or not they have made a commitment otherwise. Ask men for examples of this (e.g., have they ever told themselves they'll "never do that again" but find themselves repeating the same patterns?). Let men know that it may not be possible to alter their initial feelings. However, if they become aware of their feelings, they can alter their thoughts and ultimately change their behaviors.

Emphasize that this exercise is about teaching men to handle situations by focusing on, and gaining insight, into their own feelings, thoughts and behaviors rather than trying to control others.

Exercise 2: Thoughts and Beliefs to Watch Out For (30 min)

Let men know that we are going to practice recognizing healthy and unhealthy thoughts with a video clip.

Show a video clip. Have men identify negative thoughts and speculate on how these thoughts may prompt or justify the father's unhealthy and abusive behavior.

Give men the handout "Thoughts and beliefs to watch out for" as a concrete list of thoughts that are common precursors to abusive behavior. Review this worksheet in the group. Examples of harmful thoughts identified in this worksheet include:

- If my child respected me, he/she would listen to me
- My child is ... stubborn, stupid, defiant, spoiled, etc.
- My child should know better by now - he or she is doing this to get me
- If my child's mother would just ... than this wouldn't happen

Homework (10 min)

For homework this week, men are asked to track their thoughts in difficult situations. Men are asked to specifically describe two times that they are frustrated or upset with their child and to list the thoughts that they are having in those times.

Men also continue to complete their fathering log over the week.

Session 9: How Are Children Different From Adults?

Goal: To increase men's awareness of child-centered fathering

Exercises and Handouts	Content of Exercise
Check-in and Homework Review (40 min)	Have men check in briefly with a feeling and with any critical events from the past week. Have each man share a brief example from their homework. In particular, ask men: "What happened?" and "What did you think?" Write men's examples on the flip-chart for reference later in the group.
Exercise 1: Developmental Abilities (30 min)	Explain to men that to change their thoughts about their children, it is often helpful to have a clear understanding of children's development stages. Put men in small groups according to the approximate age of their children. Have men read through the developmental charts for children of the appropriate age. Facilitators should rotate among groups, providing feedback and examples.
Exercise 2: Practical Applications (30 min)	Instruct men to consider the examples provided during check-in. Review the Thoughts, Feelings and Behaviors triangle. For each example, groups should come up with developmentally appropriate counter thoughts to men's unhealthy thinking about the situation.
Homework Assignment (10 min)	Fathers practice consideration of their children's developmental stage.

Session 9: How Are Children Different From Adults?

Goal: To increase men's awareness of child-centered fathering

Theme: Last week, men were introduced to the idea that one way to develop healthier relationships with our children is to make our thoughts more positive. This week, facilitators begin to develop men's ability to make this shift in thinking by presenting information about children's developmental stages. There is a lot to know about developmental stages - too much for men to process in any one week. For this reason, the focus of this session is on men's understanding of one developmental stage. Men should be placed in small groups according to the age of one of their children. These small groups then work to understand the information on the developmental charts and to apply this knowledge to child behavior. This small group activity will further increase group cohesion, and will help develop men's ability to challenge and provide feedback to each other - a skill that is helpful in the weeks to come.

Materials Required for Session 9

- Developmental charts

- Worksheets: Practical applications

Check-in and Homework Review (40 min)

Invite men to check in briefly with any pressing issues from the past week (e.g., changes in access, incident with partner or children). Then have each man report on a frustrating parenting situation they identified in their homework, along with the thoughts they reported in that situation.

Write men's examples on the flip-chart for later reference.

Watch Time During Check-in

There is a lot of content to cover this week, so facilitators should be vigilant to time during men's check-ins. The purpose of this check-in is not to process the examples, but to solicit them for use later in this session. There will be a chance to come back to issues as the group continues.

Exercise 1: Developmental Stages (30 min)

The purpose of this exercise is to help men appreciate the developmental context of their children's behavior and reactions. Indicate to men that children go through a number of stages as they grow up. Underscore that in addition to the obvious physical changes in height and weight, children change cognitively, socially, and emotionally. At different ages, children think differently, have different concerns, and view the world differently.

In this next exercise, men will focus on one stage of development as a starting point for learning about these different stages. Assign men to small groups according to the age of their children (i.e., under 5 years, 5 to 8 years, 8 to 11 years, and teen years). If men have more than one child, ask them to consider the child who they have the most difficulty understanding, or the developmental stage with which they are least familiar.

Give the appropriate developmental chart to each small group. Have men read through sections one at a time and try to come up with examples of how these stages are reflected in their children's behavior. Facilitators should circulate through groups taking a supportive secondary role in group discussions. Facilitators can also be helpful by providing examples for men when they are having difficulties.

If time permits, facilitators may wish to have groups share one or two of their examples with the larger group.

PROCESS NOTES:

One of the contributors to child abuse is fathers' lack of understanding and appreciation of their children's abilities and needs. Unrealistic expectations can contribute both to physical abuse and to neglect. Many children are abused in child rearing situations that are frustrating, but common and not inconsistent with children's developmental level. For example, a child is at higher risk for being abused when they are being toilet trained and their parents believe that they have purposefully peed themselves.

It is very important that facilitators are prepared with clear examples of aspects of children's development. Facilitators should review developmental charts prior to the session so that they are prepared. In Appendix B, key points for each developmental stage are provided as an aid for facilitators. For those less familiar with developmental issues, the following websites may be useful:

www.investinkids.ca
www.childdevelopmentinfo.com/development
www.nationalcac.org/stages.html

As part of this discussion, facilitators need to emphasize that part of meeting children's needs is protecting them from adult concerns. For example, a father may have just had his hours at work cut, which will lead to considerable financial strain for the family. Help men recognize that this job stress and financial concerns are adult worries, not child worries. As such, a child should not be expected to be better or more grown-up because of these concerns. Recognizing this boundary is important because it is often during these stressful times that parents tend to expect their children to behave in ways that are beyond their developmental capabilities.

Consider developmental differences in children's relationships with their mothers

The focus of this session is clearly on children's developmental stages. However, it may still be relevant to emphasize needs that relate to the stability of the relationship between their parents. Facilitators may instruct men to consider what needs their children have for stability in their family, and to speculate on how their children's development might be compromised if they are not able to support the mother-child relationship.

Exercise 2: Practical Applications (30 min)

The purpose of this exercise is to have men apply their knowledge of developmental stages to actual situations. Ideally, this can be done using the examples from the beginning of group. Direct men to the examples on the flip chart from the beginning of the group.

Engage men in brainstorming a list of factors related to developmental stages that may be affecting their children's behaviors in these situations. Ask men to speculate on how thinking about their child's developmental stage may change men's thoughts, feelings and behaviors.

Ask men to return to their small groups and work through the examples provided. Have men share 1 or 2 examples with the larger group.

Alternative Option

Ideally, men can begin to apply their knowlege of child development to the examples from the beginning of group. However, in some groups men's examples may not be relevant, and in others, these examples may still be too difficult for men to process in a sufficiently objective manner. For this reason, worksheets are also provided that outline parenting situations and common parental misattributions. Men are asked to provide alternative, more developmentally appropriate, interpretations of child behaviors.

Homework (10 min)

For homework this week, ask men to complete (or continue) the developmental worksheet situations. For each situation, men should suggest a developmentally appropriate interpretation of the situation. Men should use the developmental charts for this exercise and should only be assigned the worksheet that corresponds to the stage that they considered in their small-group work.

GOAL 3:

To increase men's awareness of, and responsibility for, abusive and neglectful fathering behaviors and their impact on children

General Notes

Goal 3: To increase men's awareness of, and responsibility for, abusive, and neglectful fathering behaviors and their impact on children

The third goal, which spans sessions 10 to 14, focuses on the nature and impact of abuse and neglect. In some respects, all of the previous work has been leading to these critical sessions. However, even if men have developed more appropriate attitudes and skills for meeting childrens needs, they still need to take responsibility for their past behavior. Responsibility taking sends a powerful message to the children and women involved in men's lives. A thorough understanding of abuse dynamics also makes it more likely that men will be able to recognize and avoid these patterns in the future. Saying "I won't do it again" may reflect good intentions, but without insight into the types of thinking that lead to abuse and the ability to recognize more subtle forms of abuse, men are unlikely to be successful in making significant and lasting changes to their behavior. There are two main strategies used to achieve these difficult goals – clear understanding of child maltreatment and effective confrontation.

Key therapeutic skills for this section include:

1. Understanding child maltreatment

A critical foundation for increasing men's understanding of abuse is helping men develop a broader sense of what constitutes child maltreatment. The legal concept of child abuse is defined by discrete acts of child maltreatment that meet a certain legal threshold. The *Caring Dads* program addresses a much broader range of negative parenting behaviors. It also attempts to highlight the importance of ongoing *patterns* that might not meet the legal threshold for any one behavior, but that constitute harm to children when combined. For facilitators to be able to foster this more comprehensive concept of child maltreatment, they need to have a very clear conception of child maltreatment.

In *Caring Dads*, child maltreatment is broadly defined as the "*repeated use of parenting strategies that diminish children's sense of themselves as individuals worthy of love and respect.*" This broad definition, along with the parent- to child-centered continuum and the Not Valuing Children wheel, should be used as an internal guide for facilitators in considering behaviors that are, and are not, abusive.

In helping the group to generate examples of abuse and having men speculate on why these examples are abusive, it is helpful for facilitators to tie parent behavior back to children's needs. By our definition, a behavior may be abusive when it focuses on parents' needs to the exclusion of meeting children's needs. The following list of dynamics that can lead to maltreatment are provided to facilitate this discussion.

a. Fear and intimidation

It is important for children to respect, but not fear, their parents. When parents behave in ways that create fear, they are most often looking for a short-cut to getting children to behave in ways that they want.

b. Lack of security

To grow and develop in a healthy way, children need to have security. They need t feel their father is predictable and safe. They also need a sense of security in the relationships among the people who love them. A major threat to this sense of security is men's abuse of children's mothers.

c. Lack of attention

To learn about themselves, children need the feedback of those who love them. One of a parent's most important roles is to provide this feedback by mirroring their child's feelings - to take delight in what their children delight in, to recognize and help them figure out when they are tired or sad. When parents do not pay attention to their children, do not know their children, or are too wrapped up in their own needs and concerns, they don't give children the attention that they need to grow up in healthy ways.

d. Disruption of innocence

An important job of parents is to allow children to preserve their innocence for long enough to develop the skills they need to handle the world. When children have to take care of their parents or worry about adult problems they cannot focus on being a child. For example, a child who is worried about whether her father will hurt her mother will have difficulty meeting the academic and social demands of school. This disruption of innocence also happens when parents expose children to things that are beyond their ability to understand, such as adult sexuality, violence or criminal behavior or when children are given too much independence and expected to learn skills that are beyond their abilities.

e. Lack of support

Parents are the people who children rely on to love them, care for them, and have a positive view of them. If parents give up on their children, their children will give up on themselves too. Similarly, if parents start to see their children negatively, or get into the habit of thinking about them in a consistently negative way, children will begin to see themselves in this way.

f. Lack of independence and insufficient time to try new skills

There are so many skills and lessons to be learned between childhood and adulthood. Younger children need to learn to tie their own shoes, feed and dress themselves. Older children need to learn how to find their way from place to place and how to spend money. Allowing children to learn these skills takes time and patience from parents because children, like all people first learning something, require a lot of time. When parents are consistently too busy or rushed or inattentive to take this time to allow children to learn, children end up facing the world feeling incompetent and unskilled.

g. Especially rigid gender expectations

Some men hold especially rigid gender expectations of their children. Such expectations are harmful to the extent that fathers withdraw support from their children when they do not meet these expectations. This withdrawal sends a clear and harmful message to children that their father's love and support is conditional.

2. Confrontation

Confrontation (also known as challenging) is one of the most misunderstood techniques in the counselling process. The very term suggests hostility and conflict. However, if done correctly, confrontation is a very effective tool. Effective confrontation is done within the context of a supportive and respectful therapist-client relationship and strong group cohesion (which is why we do not start confrontation earlier in the program). The success with which the first goal was achieved will directly affect the work that is done in this section. Confrontation can focus on providing feedback or on identifying discrepancies. The following sections identify common situations in which confrontation is appropriate.

a. Feedback confrontation for responsibility

One goal of feedback confrontation is to help men take full responsibility for their abusive behavior. This level of responsibility is necessary for men to move beyond their currently unhealthy behavior and towards more nurturing fathering. It is also necessary so that men are able to take responsibility for their abuse while talking to their children and potentially their partner about their behavior and its impact.

We are aiming for men to be able to say: "I understand that my actions were my choice and that what I did was wrong." To get men to this point, it is often necessary to challenge some key self-deception statements. The following are types of statements that facilitators should be on the lookout for and should confront.

depersonalization – occurs when men speak of their behavior in third person. For example, a man may talk about "when the violence happened" (instead of "when I slapped her"). Men also depersonalize the situation by avoiding the use of the names of their victims (e.g., "I guess she saw me", rather than "Jennifer saw me").

rationalization – occurs when fathers are unable to speak of their actions without adding a "but" and without a long story to rationalize their behavior. For example, a father may talk about a time when he was busy with work and essentially lost track of his child for a month. A father could take responsibility for this choice by thinking about the impact his behavior may have had on his child and by considering other options. Alternatively, he might go into a long explanation of why he had no choice about his behavior. This rationalization should be explored by facilitators and potentially challenged. Was this really his only choice?

blaming – blaming is another form of rationalization. Fathers often blame either their children or their partners for their hostile, controlling, abusive or neglectful behavior. For example a father may say: "I did yell at my child for a long time. I guess it was over the top. But, I know my son, and it would not have sunk in if I didn't let him know that I was really serious about this." We want men to stop at the "over the top" part – not go on to rationalize or justify their behavior. Instead we want, "My behavior was over the top and I could have handled this situation in a different way."

b. Feedback confrontation for empathy

A second form of feedback confrontation typically used in *Caring Dads* is to challenge men to consider more fully the impact of their behavior on their children and female partners.

minimization – minimization is any statement or action that makes less of the seriousness or impact of a particular behavior. This defense is very common among the clients of the program. Things to listen for are the use of the word "just" or "only", as in: "I just hit her once" or "I only confided in her about my problems with her mother a few times – I don't know why it is such a big deal." These types of statements make light of the abusive behavior. Facilitators should pick up on these minimizations and address them by talking about the function of this type of language. Facilitators also counter minimization by clearly labeling abusive behavior as abuse, not as "the thing you did" or "when you did that." Finally, focusing on the impact of the behavior on the child, rather than on the rationalization, will help men develop more empathy.

using humor to make light of abuse - both men and facilitators will make use of humor during group and this is generally a very good tool. However, facilitators must remain aware of when and how such humor is used. In particular, men may sometimes use humor to make light of their own behavior or situation. For example, after hearing one man's story, another client commented, in a joking way "well, of course he acted like a pig, what else is he supposed to do when he is hog-tied like that?", resulting in laughter from the entire group. In cases like this, facilitators should point out the inappropriate use of humor (which in this case also involves blaming). They may also ask men to reflect on the impact this comment might have had on the victim of that man's abuse had she been in the room when the joke was made.

reframes to avoid personal responsibility – this situation is often encountered in cases where men have negative and hostile feelings towards the children's mother and reframe group material to be about her. For example, during the brainstorm of abuse examples, men may come up with examples of things that their partners have done, rather than things that they have done. When men reframe like this, they are often looking for justification for their own anger and negative opinions. Facilitators should be aware of this possibility and be ready to challenge men. Facilitators may ask men directly if the example behavior is something that they have done or something that their partner has done. If men indicate that the latter is the case, it is useful to spend time challenging men about why they are using their partner's examples rather than their own. Facilitators can make the point that focusing on the behavior of others only serves to increase blaming and anger and divert men from examining and taking responsibility for their own behavior.

c. Confrontation about inconsistent information

This powerful type of confrontation is most often used to challenge men about inconsistency between their purported intentions (e.g., "I just want my kids to tell me what is going on in their lives") and behaviors (e.g., incidences of ridicule and humiliation when children shared personal information). This type of confrontation can be empowering for men if done genuinely by facilitators. Men often repeat cycles from the past. For example, one man was caught up in extremely hostile feelings towards his children's mother and, as a result, was neglectful of his children's emotional needs. This same man was abandoned by his father when he was a child and was firmly committed to not doing the same thing to his children. In this case, facilitators were able to point out the incongruity between his commitment to be with his children, and the fact that he was currently ignoring their needs. This pairing of feedback helps men focus on their strengths and ideals instead of on blaming and rationalizing their behavior.

d. Other considerations about confrontation

In a well-functioning group, men will also begin to challenge and confront each other's intentions and the impact of their behaviors on their children. Facilitators can help this process along by:

- Asking men to offer feedback about a particular situation a man is describing.

- Asking men to speculate on the potential impact of a behavior

- Asking if other men in the group have similarly minimized or blamed and have come though it to fuller responsibility.

Finally, timing should be a consideration. Confrontation should be conducted when there will be ample time to process the challenge and come to a resolution. A major challenge as men are leaving the session may leave the group feeling unsettled, angry or frustrated rather than motivated to change.

Session 10: Recognizing Unhealthy, Hurtful, Abusive And Neglectful Fathering Behaviors

Goal: To increase men's awareness of, and responsibility for, abusive and neglectful fathering behaviors and their impact on children

Exercises and Handouts	Content of Exercise
Check-in (15 min)	Have men check in briefly with a feeling and with any critical events from the past week.
Exercise 1: Review (25 min)	In the past few weeks, two important concepts have been covered: 1) the thoughts, feelings, actions triangle and 2) developmental stages. Facilitators should review these two concepts.
Exercise 1: Decision point Option 1. What's Your Style (60 min)	Using the "What's your style" handout, have men place themselves in either the negative, positive or neutral categories for attitudes toward others. Chart using the parenting continuum.
Option 2. At the Other End of the Parenting Continuum (40 min)	Put the parenting continuum back up at the front of the room and have men brainstorm a list of behaviors that clearly fall at the abusive end of the continuum.
Exercise 2: Application of Knowledge (20-40 min)	To solidify men's knowledge of abuse, it is helpful for them to apply this knowledge to an interaction. Facilitators should show men the assigned video clip and ask them to identify abusive behaviors that they see.
Homework (10 min)	For homework this week, fathers are asked to make a list of three things they have done that have been abusive towards their children.

Session 10: Recognizing Unhealthy, Hurtful, Abusive And Neglectful Fathering Behaviors

Goal: To increase men's awareness of and responsibility for abusive and neglectful fathering behaviors and their impact on children

Theme: Until this point, the focus has been mainly on teaching positive relationship skills. However, to meaningfully effect change, it is also necessary to directly challenge men's abusive behaviors. The goal for this session is to have men come to an understanding of the nature of child abuse. There are two main approaches that facilitators can take. One involves men reflecting on their personal style and then applying it to the parenting continuum. The other is more educationally focused and involves a straight brainstorm of different forms of parent-centered abusive behaviors. The group then moves on to viewing and analyzing a video clip depicting forms of abuse.

Materials Required for Session 10

- Worksheet: Not Valuing Children Wheel

- Video clip

Check-in (15 min)

Men should briefly check in with how they are feeling and any critical events from the past week.

Exercise 1: Review (25 min)

Facilitators should review the thoughts, feelings, behaviors triangle and developmental stages to ensure men's understanding. Ask men what they learned from discussions of these concepts. Key points to review include that thoughts affect both feelings and behaviors and that children greatly differ in their abilities as they grow. Link these concepts together by explaining that men's thoughts about their children's development will affect their feelings and behaviors towards their children.

Remind men that we started this set of lessons a few weeks ago with the idea that there are sometimes barriers to listening to, nurturing, and building relationships with our children. We have now covered three important barriers – negative thoughts, a lack of appreciation for children's developmental stage, and conflictual relationships with other important people in children's lives.

Exercise 1: Decision Point

Facilitators now need to make a decision on how best to approach defining abusive, parent-centered behaviors. For groups that tend to be more open and self-reflective, we suggest that facilitators begin with the "What's your style?" exercise, listed as Option 1. For groups that are less self-reflective, it may be better to begin with Option 2 which is a more educational and impersonal exercise.

Option 1: What's Your Style? (60 min)

Put four columns on the flip chart as follows and explain to men that they are going to rate themselves in the negative, positive, or neutral categories for attitudes toward others, mood, and outlook. Facilitators should chart men's responses in the following manner:

	Attitude Towards Others	Mood	Outlook
John	negative	negative	neutral
Steve	neutral	positive	neutral

Ask men to speculate on the kind of fathering actions that they are likely to use given their style, and about the likely impact of those behaviors on children. For example, if a father has a largely negative attitude towards others, he is likely to see his child as out to get him and to punish him or her harshly. This harsh parenting is likely to make the child feel guilty and afraid.

As this exercise is being completed, facilitators should chart men's responses on the parenting continuum. For example, if John's attitudes and mood are mostly negative, where are his actions likely to fall on the continuum of parent-centered to child-centered behaviors?

After completing this exercise, it is likely that there will be many intermediate points labeled on the parenting continuum, but few extreme points labeled. Ask men to identify behaviors that would fall at the far end of the parenting continuum. These should include behaviors such as physical abuse, sexual abuse, abandonment, etc.

Review the Not Valuing Children wheel in men's workbooks as reference for this discussion. See process notes on Option 2 for more guidance.

PROCESS NOTES:

There may be times when a man's self-rating of his style diverges greatly from facilitators' perceptions. It this occurs, it is prudent to gently challenge men, using observations from group if possible (e.g., "You say that you have a primarily positive attitude towards others, but in this group, we've mostly heard negative attitudes about your children and partner"). This gives the father some feedback and also an opportunity to explain why his presentation in group may differ from his presentation at home or elsewhere.

Option 2: At the Other End of the Parenting Continuum (40 min)

Put the parenting continuum up at the front of the room. Have men brainstorm a list of types of behaviors that clearly fall at the abusive/parent-centered end of the continuum. Men typically generate *physical abuse* and *sexual abuse*. They will likely need to be prompted for *neglect*. When men generate the term *emotional abuse* ask them to be more specific.

As headings are generated have men provide specific examples of parenting behaviors that fall under this category. In addition, for each behavior, challenge men to provide an explanation of how this behavior is abusive. For example, ask men: "Why is this behavior at the abuse end of the continuum?" Overall, you are looking to have men generate all titles and examples on the Not Valuing Children wheel.

Next, ask men to brainstorm the impact of these behaviors on children. Prompt men for short and long-term consequences as well as impact in different domains – e.g., psychological, impact on future relationships, impact on school achievement.

Ask men to turn to the Not Valuing Children Wheel as a reference for this discussion.

PROCESS NOTES:

During this exercise, it is critical that facilitators push men to be as specific and as concrete as possible when coming up with example of abuse. For example, if a man reports that "not spending enough time with his child" is neglectful, ask him to provide a specific example of what "not spending enough time" would look like.

When possible, challenge men to personalize their examples by taking responsibility for their own behavior. For example, if a man reports that scaring a child by standing over him and yelling at him is abusive, ask him if he has done this in the past, or if this has been done to him. This type of personalization is especially important when men appear to have a good deal invested in their answer.

Also note that it is important that facilitators avoid, to the extent possible, arguing with men about whether a particular behavior is abusive. When these questions arise, a better option is to have the group respond. This way, the group can argue itself into a more inclusive definition of child maltreatment. If men disagree on whether certain behaviors are or are not clearly at the abuse end of the continuum, facilitators can be flexible. For example, they may say something like: "Joel, for you, being too busy to listen to your child when she first arrives home from school is definitely parent-centered, as you have learned that your daughter really values this time and feels ignored if you do not make time for her right then. David, for you, it is a bit different because your son Tom has a history of being direct and assertive about when he wants to talk. So for you, being busy after school is not an issue. This is an example of how the same behavior can be on different places on the continuum for different fathers and children. Joel, for you, we might place it closer to the abuse end, and for you David, we might place it more near the middle." Facilitators can contrast these more moderately parent-centered behaviors with examples of overt physical or sexual abuse that are clearly placed at the extreme end of the continuum.

Responding to Challenging Questions

It is common during this exercise for men to ask about whether a specific behavior is or is not abusive. There is almost always another agenda to this question! When faced with this situation, facilitators should consider the following:

- First, why is the client is asking this question? Is this an issue that he was investigated for? Is this a question he has about his own behavior?

- Second, consider whether there is there sufficient time in group to fully analyze the question. Generally, responding to this type of question requires gathering an understanding of the context of the situation and of men's actions. Facilitators can ask themselves: "Is this a good use of time at this point in the group? Is this a good client/example to work with?"

  - If no: If facilitators decide that this is not a good time to work through this issue, it is likely best to reflect the client's question back to him. Let him know that during the next few weeks, there will be more discussion aimed toward fully understanding the nature of abuse, and that he will gain clarity on this over time.

  - If yes: If facilitators decide to deal with this issue during the group, they can use the thoughts, feelings, and behavior triangle to process the example. Have men identify their feelings and thoughts and decide whether they are likely to lead to nurturing behavior. Then challenge men to place the behavior in question at the appropriate place on the continuum of parent-centered and child-centered behaviors.

Abuse of Children's Mothers

Be sure to include abuse of others close to children as a form of child maltreatment. Include a large range of behaviors. For example, if men in the group are using the court system to get back at their children's mothers, or are refusing to pay child support in revenge, include these behaviors on the list of parent-centered actions.

Exercise 2: Application of Knowledge (20 to 40 min)

The purpose of this exercise is to give men practice at identifying different forms of abuse. For this activity, we have often used a clip from the movie Billy Elliot; however, other videos can be used as well as long as they depict father-perpetrated child maltreatment.

Have men identify the abuse that is depicted in this video. Be sure to identify examples both obvious and more subtle forms of abuse. Faciltators then have men identify the thoughts and feelings of the abusive parent and the needs of children portrayed. If Billy Elliot is chosen, forward the video to the scene where Billy's father first finds out that he is doing ballet and confronts him about this. Abusive behaviors that are depicted include:

- The generally threatening demeanor of Billy's father
- Limiting Billy's autonomy ("you will not do ballet")
- The implication that Billy is less of a person for doing ballet
- Ignoring and yelling at Billy's Nana
- Physically pushing Billy against the wall

Also, ask men the following questions:

- What is Billy's father thinking in this situation?
- What is Billy's father feeling?
- Why did Billy state that he hated his father?
- How is Billy feeling in this situation?
- What does Billy need in this situation?

This video clip provides facilitators with an excellent opportunity to address the influence of gender stereotypes on potential for abuse. Billy's father is likely thinking that "boys don't do ballet and I am going to look like a horrible father if I allow this to happen" and may be concerned that ballet will lead to homosexuality. Facilitators may ask men to speculate on how Billy's father is feeling in this movie and what he is worried about in regard to how he may look to others.

Homework (10 min)

Explain to men that we are now asking them to engage in the difficult task of looking at some of their own behaviors that fall at the parent centered and abusive end of the parenting continuum. For homework, men are asked to list three examples of ways that they have used unhealthy parent-centered strategies with their children. For fathers who are abusive or disrespectful towards their children's mother, ensure that one example is from this relationship.

10

Session 11: How Am I Responding To My Children's Needs?

Goal: To increase men's awareness of, and responsibility for, abusive and neglectful fathering behaviors and their impact on children

Exercises and Handouts	Content of Exercise
Check-in and Homework Review (30 min)	Invite men to check in with an example of a time when they used parent-centered fathering in their relationship with their child or children.
Exercise 1: Decision point Option 1: Emotional Abuse and Neglect: Problem-Solving Example (30 min)	Show men a video clip and review forms of emotional abuse and neglect depicted. Using the video as an example, take men through the Problem-Solving for Parents steps: 1) situation; 2) intention - child or parent needs?; 3) thoughts, feelings, actions triangle; 4) effects and; 5) alternatives.
Option 2: Insults are Not Motivational (40 minutes)	Ask men to come up with examples of times in the recent past that they were made to feel alone, humiliated or rejected. Detail how men felt and make the point that children feel the same way- that insults are humiliating, not motivational. Using an example for a man in the group, review the Problem-Solving for Parents steps.
Option 3: Procede Directly to Exericse 2	If the group is quite advanced, facilitators should also feel free to move directly to a consideration of men's individual issues (Exercise 2).
Exercise 2: Personal Application of Problem-Solving for Parents (20-60 min)	Choose one of the men in group who has been making fairly good progress and who struggles with issues of emotional abuse or neglect. With the group, have this father work through the Problem-Solving for Parents steps.
Exercise 3: Alternatives to Parent-Centered and Abusive Behaviors (10 min)	In each of the above exercises, men are asked to generate alternative ways of managing their child's behavior. Facilitators should begin a list of strategies that men generate. This list will be expanded upon in subsequent weeks.
Homework (10 min)	Men are assigned the Problem-Solving for Parents steps as homework.

Session 11: How Am I Responding To My Children's Needs?

Goal: To increase men's awareness of, and responsibility for, abusive and neglectful fathering behaviors and their impact on children

Theme: The next four sessions of *Caring Dads* are devoted to understanding and challenging patterns of abuse in each man's relationship with his children. Each session, exercises are suggested to introduce a particular topic area. A framework for thinking about problematic situations is introduced and then used repeatedly to analyze men's situations. In preparation for these sessions, it is useful for facilitators to review their understanding of each man's relationships with his family and discuss the abuse dynamic that is most concerning. Then, they can track progress over the next weeks to ensure that each man has been given some group time for his issue. The materials presented in these sessions are meant to aid in the processing of men's issues. Facilitators should be flexible in their use of exercises and make modifications and/or additions if necessary so that each man's issues are appropriately addressed. Here is a chart that may help plan for this process.

Session Number	Main Issue	Client to be Challenged
Session 11	Emotional abuse and neglect	
Session 12	Intimidation and control	
Session 13	Exposure of children to the abuse of their mother	
Session 14	Minimization and denial	

Materials Required for Session 11

- Video if this option is chosen

- Flip chart paper for keeping an ongoing record of examples of alternative methods to manage child misbehavior

Check-in and Homework Review (30 min)

Facilitators should begin by asking men to briefly review last session's discussion of forms of parent-centered behaviors and abuse. Then facilitators should invite men to check in with an example of a situation in which they responded to their child in a parent-centered or abusive manner. Ask men to specifically discuss what actions they took and what they were hoping for as an outcome.

PROCESS NOTES:

During these next few sessions, check-ins serve an important function. For one, they allow facilitators to remain focused on the issues that arise for men. Second, they allow men a chance to process their changing thoughts (and hopefully behaviors) with the group.

Facilitators should be planful and flexible in their use of material over the next few sessions. A variety of exercises and videos are suggested. As stated, the main goal of these sessions is for men to be challenged on their use of abusive behavior. Videos are often helpful in this regard, as they provide a concrete display of abuse. Role plays can also be used. Alternatively, if men's examples are sufficiently rich, no other materials may be needed. Facilitators need to choose exercises and activities that will best meet the goal of challenging men about their abusive behavior.

Exercise 1: Decision Point (0-40 min)

Three exercise options are suggested for the introduction of emotional abuse and the Problem Solving for Parents steps. In the first, men are shown a video and are asked to work together through the Problem-Solving for Parents steps. This exercise is a good choice for groups that do not seem to have a clear understanding of emotionally abusive behavior or who are hesitant to provide examples of problematic fathering. The second exercise has men consider the use of insults as a motivational tool, and argues that such insults are not motivational but emotionally abusive. This exercise is most useful in groups that are struggling to adapt an empathic perspective on their children's experiences of emotional abuse. Finally, the third exercise has one man in the group work though a personal example of emotionally abusive behavior using the Problem-Solving for Parents steps. This exercise should be used in groups that have been making steady progress and whose members have a fairly good understanding of emotionally abusive parenting.

Option 1: Emotional Abuse and Neglect: Problem-Solving Example

Show a video clip depicting father-perpetrator emotional abuse. Have men identify incidents of emotional abuse in the video shown.

Once men have identified abusive behaviors, have them speculate on the intentions of the father in the video. What is the father hoping for? Ask men to speculate - is this a reasonable intention? Often, it is possible to identify a benign intention or hope as very few fathers abuse their children with the specific intention to harm them.

A short jump from intentions is the Thinking component of the Thoughts,

Feelings, Actions triangle. Draw the triangle on the board and have men list the likely thoughts the father depicted in the video. Then have men list his feelings.

Remind men that we need to look very carefully at thoughts. Make the point that we already know that these are not all healthy thoughts because we have seen the abusive actions that have resulted in this case.

Next ask men to identify the effects of these actions on the child. Have men discuss if the father's actions are likely to lead to healthy child-centered fathering or unhealthy parent-centered fathering.

At the end, you should have one (or two) sheets that look something like this:

Situation: In response to Evan's shoplifting, his father tells him that with behavior like that, he is not wanted as part of the family.

Intention: For Evan to stop stealing and behave better.

Is this intention about child needs or parent needs?: Both. Evan's antisocial behavior is problematic for both him and his father

What are the thoughts and feelings of Evan's father?

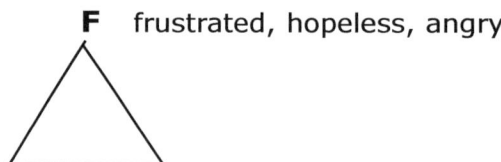

F frustrated, hopeless, angry

A   **T** Maybe this will scare some sense into the kid

Effects on the child: Evan feels alone, humiliated, rejected, hopeless, unloved, futile. These feelings are not likely to lead to any long-term improvement in behavior.

Alternatives: Let Evan know that although he may be charged by the police (a natural consequence), he will still be a part of the family and that his father will stand behind him.

Option 2: Insults are Not Motivational

Sometimes, men have difficulty understanding that feeling alone, humiliated, and rejected is unlikely to increase a child's motivation to do better. For example, men might state that: "children are fundamentally lazy and you need to push them into shape", or "none of these positive things are going to motivate my child." This exercise addresses these beliefs. Let men know that the group is going to come back to the question of whether or not these statements are motivational after a short exercise.

Part 1

Ask men to come up with examples of times in the recent past that someone insulted them. Ask for specific examples of things that people said (e.g., "you are just a jerk"). Note that it is important to use the recent past because men sometimes reinterpret events from much earlier depending upon their outcome.

Part 2

Ask men to respond to the question, "How do you feel about the person who said that to you?"

The resulting list of feelings should include affects such as: anger, distrust, insulted, distant. Ask men if as a result of being made to feel (alone, humiliated, rejected, insulted) did they feel motivated? Want to be the best that they could be? Want to be closer to the person who said this to them?

Part 3

Apply this lesson to children. Contrast men's experience with their hopes to motivate their children.

Point out that sometimes we have a double set of beliefs - we think that insults are a good motivational strategy for children, but not adults. Children, like adults, feel angry, and insecure, and humiliated when insulted. They do not feel motivated. In fact, negative and hurt feelings are even more pronounced with children because the person insulting them is a parent who is supposed to care for and love the child no matter what.

Facilitators should make the points that with children:

- The impact of insults can be worse than for adults.
- Insults are likely to make them feel helpless, because there are fewer ways to fight back. Generally, the only action that children can take is to blow off the insult and pretend it didn't matter.
- Insults weaken the child's bond with their parent.
- Children who are often insulted may use their father's insulting behavior as an example for other relationships, and insult others like teachers or friends.
- Insults can act as a self-fulfilling prophesy.
- Insults can result in hostility, aggression or depression. Sometimes when chil dren are faced with this kind of insult they act out (i.e., attack others) and sometimes children turn upon themselves (i.e., think that it must be true) and become anxious and depressed.

Part 4

Review and consolidate this lesson using an example from one man in the group. Ask the man to talk about a time that he called his child "lazy" or some other insulting name to attempt to motivate him or her. Go through the following problem solving steps. The result may appear something like this:

Situation: Tom wants to motivate his son John to do his homework so he tells him if he continues to be lazy and doesn't shape up, he is going to fail out of school and amount to nothing.

Intention: For John to complete his homework.

Is this intention about child needs or parent needs?: Both. Tom is right, John does need to complete his homework to meet his potential in school.

What are Tom's thoughts and feelings?

F frustrated, hopeless, angry

A **T** Maybe he will finally understand and get to work

Effects on John: John feels humiliated by his father and betrayed that his father would have such a low opinion of him. He is angry at being called lazy. These feelings are not likely to lead to any long-term improvement in behavior.

Alternatives: Stop thinking of Tom as lazy. Remember that one of the jobs as a parent is to help children get into good habits. Arrange things so that John will feel motivated to do his work - offer to help, or to play a game together when he has finished his work.

PROCESS NOTES:

In doing this exercise, men often rely on their own experiences of being motivated through insults. Acknowledge that there are occasions when insults "work." However, challenge men to consider whether there may have been a better way for the other person to motivate them and to speculate on any negative impact that the insult may have had. Also point out that there is a big difference in being insulted once, and being repeatedly insulted. It is repeated or extreme insults that are most likely to be harmful.

Option 3: Move directly to Exercise 2

If the group is quite advanced and does not need a review of emotional abuse, faciliators should feel free to move directly to an examination of men's individual issues.

Exercise 2: Personal Application of Problem-Solving Paradigm (20-60 min)

Complete the Problem-Solving for Parents question using an example of one of the situations that men brought to group. For this first time, it is usually best for facilitators to choose a man who is making good progress, who can be a good model for the group, and who is struggling with issues around emotional abuse or neglect of his child.

Go through the following questions. If time, repeat with a second client.

- What is the situation?

- What was your intention?

- Thinking of the parent-centered to child-centered continuum, is this intention sufficiently child-centered? **Note** - if men's intentions are identifed as being parent-centered, then the example can be stopped and men can talk about alternative, child-centered, intentions.

- What were your thoughts, feelings and actions?

- What was the effect on your child? Contrast effects with intentions.

- What are alternative thoughts and actions? **Note** - if facilitators are struggling with altertnatives, they can review the set of general options provided in Session 16.

Time permitting, repeat these problem-solving steps with other clients.

Situation:

Intention:

Child needs or parent needs:

Thoughts, feelings, and actions:

Effects on child:

Alternatives:

Responding to Challenges

Sometimes during this exercise, the group will assert that abuse is the only way to handle a given situation. Strategies to deal with this include:

- Asking the man who is the focus of the example - "Is this issue something that is happening over and over again in your relationship with your child?" If yes, point out it is apparent that what he is doing is not working, or he wouldn't still be having this issue.

- Asking men in the group: "What are indicators that things are not going so well, that maybe he isn't doing the right thing?"

- Asking the group: "How will he know that he is on the right track? How will his child feel? What will their relationship be like?"

Exercise 3: Alternatives to Parent-Centered and Abusive Behaviors (10 min)

Ask men to review alternatives to parent-centered and abusive behaviors that were generated during discussions this session. Ensure that alternatives are listed on a separate page that can be added to in subsequent sessions. In Session 16, the group will return to this list of alternatives to parent-centered and abusive behaviors for review and for more in depth consideration.

Homework (10 min)

Assign the Problem-Solving for Parents steps as homework. Let each man know that he will need to present his example to the group. Facilitators may consider giving men a few minutes to write down an example situation before they leave so that they can provide feedback about the appropriateness of men's choice of problem-solving situations. Men also continue to keep their fathering log.

Session 12: Relationship With My Child's Mother

Goal: To increase men's awareness of, and responsibility for, abusive and neglectful fathering behaviors and their impact on children

Exercises and Handouts	Content of Exercise
Check-in and Homework Review (40 min)	Facilitators may wish to have men review their homework in pairs prior to check-in as a way to increase men's comfort. Invite men to check in and follow-up with any man who has worked through his Problem-Solving for Parents example with the group.
Exercise 2: Decision Point (30 min) Option 1: How Children are Affected by Witnessing Abuse of Their Mother	Show a video clip about domestic violence. Discuss men's reactions to the video and have men brainstorm potential effects of the abuse on the child.
Option 2: Parent-Child Boundaries	Discuss the distinction between adult problems and child problems and about the importance of maintaining appropriate boundaries between them. An example is provided to clarify this issue.
Option 3: Involvement in the Legal System	Help men appreciate the differences between asserting legal rights, and using the legal system for retribution against a partner. Have men problem-solve with examples of child-centered and parent-centered legal involvement.
Exercise 3: Personal Application of Problem-Solving Paradigm (30 min)	Invite men to share their homework examples with the group. Each man should go through the problem-solving steps: 1) situation; 2) intention - child or parent needs?; 4) thoughts, feelings, actions triangle; 5) effects; 6) alternatives. The group should be used to support this process. This session, facilitators should specifically involve men with examples involving abuse of children's mother or use of the justice system for retribution against their partner.
Homework (10 min)	Men are assigned the fathering log and the Problem-Solving for Parents steps as homework.

Session 12: Relationship With My Child's Mother

Goal: To increase men's awareness of, and responsibility for, abusive and neglectful fathering behaviors and their impact on children

Theme: This week, facilitators address men's relationships with their children's mothers and other important people in their children's lives. Facilitators can choose to focus on the impact of witnessing domestic violence, the importance of good boundaries around parental conflict or men's involvement in the legal system. In all cases, the message to men is that to be a good father to their children, they must also have non-abusive relationships with other people who are important to their children, in particular, with children's mothers.

Materials Required for Session 12

- Worksheet: Myths and facts: How children are affected by parental conflict

- Video clip, if this option is chosen

Check-in and Homework Review (40 min)

Ask men to check in with examples of abusive or parent-centered parenting that they have used in the past week. Be sure to specifically follow-up with men who have shared their examples with the group in previous weeks to review on men's progress in behaving in healthier and more nurturing ways. Depending on the cohesiveness of the group, it is sometimes helpful to begin this process by having men share their problem-solving homework in pairs prior to checking in with the whole group. This small group work may offset some of the anxiety men feel about sharing examples of their abusive behaviors.

Exercise 2: Decision Point (30 min)

Three exercise options are provided to introduce this session's material, and facilitators again need decide which exercise is most relevant to the men in the group. Groups who wish to focus on the impact of children witnessing abuse of their mother should choose exercise Option 1. In this exercise, men watch and process a short video of a child witnessing his father's abuse of his mother. If members of a group have a good understanding of the impact of witnessing domestic violence, but still struggle with significant issues around conflict with their children's mothers, exercise Options 2 or 3 may be more appropriate. Option 2 has men focus on the importance of making the distinction between adult problems and children problems, and on keeping good parent-child boundaries around adult conflict. Option 3 has men consider when involvement in the legal system is justified and appropriate, and when such involvement is clearly parent-centered. This option is appropriate in groups where one or more members have continually drawn their partners into legal battles.

If the men in the group have very different issues with respect to their relationship with their children's mothers, it may make sense to split the group with some members doing Option 1, and others Options 2 or 3.

Option 1: How Children are Affected by Witnessing Abuse of Their Mother

This exercise focuses on developing men's empathy for the impact on children of witnessing abuse of their mother. Show men the brief video vignette of a child exposed to domestic violence (we suggest the video from the Violence Prevention Fund, www.endabuse.org). During this video, a toddler is depicted sitting on the stairs while listening to his father verbally and physically abusing his mother.

Discuss men's reactions to the video. Ask them to speculate on the age of the child in the video. Brainstorm a list of abusive behaviors used by the father in the video. Behaviors include: insulting, blaming, intimidation and physical abuse.

Then move to a brainstorm of the potential impact on the child. Important points to cover in this brainstorm include:

- Worry about his parents
- Self-blame
- Fear, anxiety, and aloneness
- Needing to grow up quickly
- Lack of sleep
- Lack of a sense of safety and security
- Confusion (as parents will likely not address this incident with the child the next day)

Also ask men to speculate on the next day. What might the impact be on this child's mother and how might it impact the child the next day?

Child's mother....
- is likely to be preoccupied and not pay attention to child
- may be tired and irritable
- may be hurt and unable to play in certain ways
- is likely to be sad
- may be overly harsh, or overly permissive with child with the worry that she doesn't want him to turn out like his father

Child may...
- try to cheer up his mother
- try to get mother's attention by misbehaving

Close this exercise with a summary of the impact of witnessing domestic violence.

If time...

Facilitators can invite men to role play a different ending to this scenario. One actor should play the man returning home from work feeling angry and disappointed that there was pizza for dinner. Another man should role play the child, sitting to the side and watching the scene. The role of the woman can be played by a third man, or by one of the facilitators. Instruct the actors to replay the scene. Once finished, have them check in with the child observer. How did the child feel in this situation? Did he feel more secure and safe and was he less likely to blame himself? If desired, repeat the scene again, with slightly different actions by each charcter (e.g., can change the reactions of the husband or wife).

But This Child is too Young to Understand

Facilitators need to be ready to deal with men's assertions that the child in this video is too young to understand, remember, or be affected by this incident. The first way to handle this challenge is to turn the question back to the group, commenting: "What do other men feel? Do you agree that, chances are, this child will not be affected?" This way, other group members consolidate their views on the impact of domestic violence. If this approach is not successful, facilitators may wish to emphasize the fact that children understand more than we think. For example, although this child may not understand the nature of the argument, he will certainly understand that something bad is happening. Children may feel that they are treading on eggshells with both parents. Also, it may be useful to emphasize that this child certainly had to calm and soothe himself. Remind men that, at this age, children rely on others for calming and soothing, and this child has perhaps already learned that there are situations where he has to rely only on himself. It can also be helpful to draw men's attention back to the way they may have felt as children when they were exposed to similar situations.

Facilitators should also be ready to address men in the group who may respond to the video with extreme anger and degradation of the father portrayed. Sensitive handling of these comments is critical as some of the men in the group may have behaved in a manner similar to the father portrayed.

Option 2: The Importance of Parent-Child Boundaries

This exercise focusess on inappropriate boundaries between fathers and children. Signs of inappropriate father-child boundaries include fathers confiding in children, having children attend to fathers' emotional needs, or using children to mediate or send messages in adult disputes.

Start by asking men to consider whether there are things that children should and should not be told. Do men confide in their children about everything, or not? How do men decide what to tell their children and what not to tell their children? Relate this back to the parenting continuum with the assertion that children should be told things if it meets their needs, not if it meets the parents needs.

Ask men to brainstorm examples of inappropriate boundaries between parents and children - examples of when confiding in children is inappropriate. Encourage men to explore personal examples of when they may have violated their children's boundaries. Examples include:

- Confiding in a child about anger at their mother
- Talking to a child about difficulties at work
- Confiding to a younger child about inability to pay family bills
- Being very open with a child about adult sexuality
- Relying on children for emotional support (e.g., child as best friend)
- Insisting children regularly understand and make allowances for your mood (e.g., having different rules when you are in a bad mood)
- Talking to children about issues that are not appropriate to their age (e.g., talking to a younger child about going on a drug run)

Make the point that these behaviors are boundary violations. In other words, they place responsibility for adult issues and problems on the child. Because children are unable to cope with these things, they get weighed down by these issues and have to grow up too quickly. Close this exercise with a summary of the need for appropriate boundaries between fathers and children.

Option 3: Child and Parent-Centered Involvement in the Legal System

This exercise focuses on men's inappropriate use of the legal system (or other systems) to punish their children's mother. An example is a very contentious divorce in which men continue to pursue action against their partners for small issues (e.g., arguing for change in custody because she was late for access visits) or call police or child protective services when they disagree with their partner's parenting choices. These are difficult cases, because it is often hard to determine what is a reasonable response and what is revenge against a partner. In past groups, we have handled this by drawing the distinction between "defensive" and "retributive" actions and by helping men to consider whether their actions are motivated by a desire to benefit their children or control the children's mother.

Put the continuum of parent and child needs up on the flip chart. Explain that the group is going to discuss how men's involvement with different systems can be parent-centered and child-centered. Have men brainstorm a list of actions on each end of the continuum.

Summarize by pointing out that when men are angry with their partners, they can sometimes convince themselves that actions taken to get back at their partner are actually in their children's best interests. Remind men that they need to carefully consider whose needs are being met before getting other systems involved, or prolonging court involvement, as the continued uncertainty of court involvement is harmful to children. When men's actions are pursued with the intent to punish a partner, get back at her that something that happened in the past, or "set the record straight", men are most likely acting in parent-centered ways. In contrast, when actions are pursued defensively or out of a genuine concern for child well-being, men are most likely acting in child-centered ways.

> **PROCESS NOTES:**
>
> *We have occasionally dealt with fathers in families where evidence suggests that the mother of their children was also struggling with her own issues and, as a result, was having significant difficulties caring for their children. For example, a mother may be drinking or using drugs while caring for children or may be negligent of their physical or emotional needs. We have found that the first approach of fathers in situations like these tends to be to try to force the children's mother to provide better care using emotionally abusive methods. Not surprisingly, these efforts often backfire and the problems get worse. At this point, many fathers withdraw from the situation and spend very little time at home, thus neglecting the children's needs. Caring Dads considers the needs of the child as primary. Therefore, in these situations, the father should be encouraged to "step up" to parenting responsibilities. Increased father responsibility can be achieved by empathizing with the father about his current situation, but then clearly locating it as an adult problem for which children should not be the ones to suffer. Men should be reminded that they have control only over their behavior, not over the behavior of their partners, so that expending energy on trying to get her to change is likely to be ineffective. Instead, men need to do what they can to meet the demands of being a parent. For example, a father could take more responsibility for ensuring that he meets his children's needs. Facilitators should draw on their experience working with single parents and with mothers who are parenting children with a mostly absent father to come up with examples of how men can deal with these difficult situations.*

Reporting Children's Mothers to Child Protective Services

In most groups, at least one father presents facilitators with concerns about the safety of the parenting choices being made by the children's mother. Often, men's anger towards their children's mother makes it difficult to judge the severity of men's concerns and even more difficult to make decisions about whether a mother's behavior warrants a report to child protective services. Although guidelines around duty to report must be followed, we also recommend that *Caring Dads* facilitators first communicate with other professionals involved with the family to gauge the context of men's reported concerns. Facilitators can then include information from collateral professionals about the siutation if they need to make a report about children's mother to child welfare.

Exercise 3: Personal Application of Problem-Solving Paradigm (30 min)

Encourage men to apply the problem-solving paradigm to their situations by using an example from one of the situations that men brought to group. Ideally, transition to this exercise should follow quite closely to the discussion of difficult situations in Exercise 2.

What is the Situation:

What was your Intention:

Is intention about Child needs or Parent needs:

Thoughts, feelings, and actions:

Effects on child:

Alternatives:

Often the alternative for these behaviors is simply to stop behaving in this way. Men can sometimes reach this point in the second problem-solving step. For example, in one of our past groups, a man reported withholding child support payments. When asked about his intentions, he revealed that he was doing this because he wanted his partner to get a job. Facilitators challenged this man about whether his behavior was relevant to his needs or his child's needs. The man was able to clearly state that his actions were motivated by his own needs and desire to change the behavior of his former partner, and were detrimental to his children. He was also able to accept feedback that he has control only over his own actions, not over the actions of his partner, and thus is unable to force her to get a job. Because his intention was clearly parent-centered, the rest of the problem-solving for parents exercise did not need to be completed. Instead, the group concluded that he should begin making child support payments.

Facilitators should remember to continue to add to the list of alternatives to parent-centered behaviors that was generated last session.

PROCESS NOTES:

For a number of men, problems are going to involve interactions with partners with whom they are no longer living. Some of the main ways that men who are separated from their children's mother abuse their children or neglect their children's needs are:

- *Contesting custody as a means of trying to hurt or harass the other parent*
- *Contesting custody without regard to children's needs and best interests*
- *Withholding visitation rights or support payments as a means of hurting the other parent*
- *Being inconsistent or irresponsible regarding visitation (i.e., picking up the child late, returning the child late or early, stopping by at non-planned times etc.)*
- *Blaming the child for fights or separation*
- *Making the mother the "bad guy" / blaming the mother / pitting the child against the mother*
- *Avoiding parenting responsibilities (e.g., enforcing rules) and instead acting only as a playmate for the child*

Homework (10 min)

Ask men to review the "Myths and Facts: How children are affected by parental conflict" handout. Men should continue the fathering log and should continue to fill out the Problem-Solving for Parents exercise.

Session 13: Problem-Solving In Difficult Situations

Goal: To increase men's awareness of, and responsibility for, abusive and neglectful fathering behaviors and their impact on children

Exercises and Handouts	Content of Exercise
Check-in (40 min)	Have men check in with a report on their past week. Be sure to follow up on problem-solving with clients who were the focus of the group's attention in the previous weeks.
Exercise 1: Personal Application of Problem-Solving Paradigm (50 min)	Invite men to share their homework examples with the group. Each man should go through the problem-solving steps: 1) situation; 2) intention - child or parent needs?; 3) thoughts, feelings, actions triangle; 4) effects; 5) alternatives. The group should be used to support this process.
Exercise 2: What Children Learn From Abusive and Controlling Fathering (10 min)	Ask men to brainstorm about what children learn from abusive and controlling fathering. Refer men to the relevant handout and briefly review it.
Homework (10 min)	Men are asked to continue practicing the Problem-Solving for Parents steps as homework.

Session 13: Problem-Solving In Difficult Situations

Goal: To increase men's awareness of, and responsibility for, abusive and neglectful fathering behaviors and their impact on children

Theme: This entire session is devoted to addressing issues of abuse being perpetrated by men in their families. For homework, men have been asked to complete the Problem-Solving for Parents steps. This is an important opportunity for challenging men to engage in more child-centered parenting. Facilitators should continue from past weeks' discussions in working through issues and problems.

Materials Required for Session 13

- Worksheet: What children learn from abusive and controlling fathering

Check-in (40 min)

Invite men to check in with a brief review of any events from the past week. During check-in, follow up with the clients who provided examples in previous weeks, and ask about use of alternative thoughts or actions.

> **PROCESS NOTES:**
>
> By tracking the progress of men from week to week, facilitators are provided with an excellent opportunity to gauge the extent to which men have been able to put group suggestions into action. Tracking men's progress is easy and rewarding when clients have found that the suggested alternative strategies have been successful. When clients have not been successful however, managing their check-ins can be more difficult. In such situations, facilitators must balance the needs of the clients who have already begun problem-solving with those who have not yet given their problem-solving examples to the group. Facilitators should avoid falling into patterns of working intensely with only one or two men. A helpful strategy is to ask men who have not been successful to identify those aspects of their problems-solving that were a little more successful (i.e., did he stay more calm?), and then to encourage positive self-talk and additional problem-solving. Inviting men to generate additional alternative thoughts and actions and to discuss them briefly with facilitators before or after group, is another way to provide support without taking too much time from the other men in the group.

Exercise 1: Personal Application of Problem-Solving Paradigm (50 min)

Complete the Problem-Solving for Parents questions used in previous weeks, using an example of one of the situations that men brought to group. Continue with examples from other men. Facilitators should remember to keep adding to the list of alternatives to parent-centered behaviors.

Situation:

Intention:

Child needs or parent needs:

Thoughts, feelings, and actions:

Effects on child:

Alternatives:

Exercise 2: What Children Learn From Abusive and Controlling Fathering (10 min)

This is likely to be an intense session with a great deal of attention focused on a few clients. For this reason, it is good to end with a short educational exercise. Give men 10 minutes to brainstorm different problems with using power and control tactics with children. Then, direct men to the relevant handout that reviews some of the problems with using adult power to force child compliance. Some examples are that:

- Children learn not to get caught
- Children learn to expect abuse from authority figures
- Children become accustomed to relying on power differences to solve disagreements
- Children learn to abuse others

Note that this educational exercise is a review designed to solidify material that has already been learned.

Homework (10 min)

Assign the Problem-Solving for Parents steps to men as homework again. Facilitators may consider leaving a few minutes at the end of the group to provide direction to those men whose original homework examples (i.e., those prepared for this session) were not appropriate and to help men who have completed one or two sets of problem-solving steps get started on a new example.

Men are also asked to continue to keep the fathering log.

Session 14: Decreasing Denial and Minimization

Goal: To increase men's awareness of, and responsibility for, abusive and neglectful fathering behaviors and their impact on children

Exercises and Handouts	Content of Exercise
Check-in (10 min)	Do a *brief* check in with men with the question: "How are you feeling tonight."
Exercise 1: Decision Point Option 1 : Shame and Secrecy (60 min)	Introduce men to the idea that things that they feel badly about and keep secret tend to fester, ultimately making situations worse. Give each man a piece of paper and ask that they give a written description of something they have done that has been very harmful to their children. Discuss the impact of this exercise, focusing on the differentiation between shame and guilt.
Option 2: Go to exercise 2	Facilitators may decide to skip discussion of shame and move directly to exercise 2.
Exercise 2: Effect of Denial on Children (10 to 20 min)	Make a transition to this short exercise on the impact of denial on children. If the group has been working through the shame exercise, this can be done by asking for an example from the discussion. If not, draw from one man's Problem-Solving for Parents homework.
Exercise 3: Problem-Solving for parents (20 to 60 min)	Using the Problem-Solving for Parents template, work through an example of how denial and minimization of abusive actions negatively impact children.
Homework (10 min)	Men are asked to spend some time thinking about the group material.

Session 14: Decreasing Denial and Minimization

Goal: To increase men's awareness of, and responsibility for, abusive and neglectful fathering behaviors and their impact on children

Theme: Facilitators face an important decision this session. One option is for the group to continue working through Problem-Solving for Parents exercises. The other is to move to a consideration of shame and its impact on abuse and healing. Careful consideration should be given to the choice of options.

Materials Required for Session 14

No materials needed this week, but it is critical that facilitators carefully review the rationale for shame work prior to beginning.

IMPORTANT RATIONALE FOR FACILITATORS

Shame is the feeling of being exposed and found lacking in dignity, self-worth, and esteem. Shame is critically important to understanding the presentation of many individuals who have been abusive. In particular, an individual's inability to tolerate (and associated desire to hide) feelings of worthlessness can give rise to many of the defensive, hostile, and angry reactions that are typical of abusive fathers. Shame also prevents men from taking responsibility for their abusive behavior because to do so would mean devaluing the entire self.

The aim of intervention for shame is for the therapist to help the client move from feeling shame about the self to feeling guilt for particular actions. In other words, the therapist's job is to support the client's self-blame for their inappropriate abusive behavior, while at the same time, countering the client's tendency to generalize regrets about specific behaviors to condemnation of the entire self. This distinction may be captured by the difference in the statements: "You should be ashamed of yourself" and "Although you behaved in a shameful way these times, I am confident that you are not shameful. You are someone who can behave in a different way in the future." By simultaneously holding a view of the client as someone who is worthy of dignity and respect and who has behaved in a way that is completely wrong and terribly hurtful to others, therapists' model a non-encompassing view of abusive actions. With this differentiation between shame and self-worth, clients can move toward taking responsibility for their behavior and developing new relationships with their children.

Supporting clients in their shame work is challenging. Facilitators are more likely to be successful if the group is relatively cohesive and ready for a high level of personal disclosure. If the group is not ready, then asking men to discuss shameful behaviors may actually increase men's shame, rather than reduce it.

Check-in and Review of Homework (10 min)

Invite men to do a *brief* check in with the question "How are you feeling right now?" and with any critical events from the past week.

If facilitators are confident about their ability to bring out and appropriately counter men's feelings of shame, Option 1 offers a powerful opportunity to do so. In this exercise, men write about a time that they have behaved in a shameful manner and then share this exerience with others in the group. If facilitators feel that the group is lacking sufficient cohesiveness or if men are not ready for shame work, it is better to skip this exerice and move move directly into a consideration of the impact of denial and minimization on children.

Option 1: Shame and Secrecy

Facilitators should begin by asking men to differentiate between guilt and shame.

Guilt is feeling badly about a particular act. It is an extremely important emotion to have because it can help prevent people from acting in ways that are harmful to themselves or others. Guilt is a social corrector of behavior. When we try to help kids understand what they did wrong, we are encouraging their experience of guilt. This is okay - children have to know what they have done wrong so they can change it. Guilt is the feeling "I have done something wrong."

Shame is feeling badly about your entire self. It is a feeling of core, inside, deep badness. We grow up sometimes with messages about ourselves as being worthless, useless, and bad. When parents are using shame-based parenting to correct children, they make children feel inadequate, useless, and bad about themselves. These stratgeis affect children's self-esteem. Shame is the feeling "I am a bad person."

Remind men that we have already talked a bit about this kind of shame when we talked about emotional abuse. Specifically, we talked about how insulting a child or trying to make them feel badly about themselves is an abusive and parent-centered parenting strategy.

Introduction

Let men know that today we are going to look at the shame that we may feel as parents. We are going to do this because if people have too much shame, they can't talk about issues, can't look themselves in the eye, isolate themselves, and sometimes feel rage because the feelings of inadequacy are overwhelming. These feelings tend to make things worse and can make it more difficult for parents to relate to their children.

Explain to men that they are going to look at their own shame this week to help them consider how they react when they feel inadequate or ashamed.

Activity

Give each man a piece of paper. Ask men to describe in writing one thing that they have done that they feel has been harmful to their children and that they've felt ashamed of. Men should be brutally honest and provide as much detail as possible in their descriptions. If men are stuck with trying to decide what to write, it is sometimes useful to talk about the bodily sensations associated with shame. For example, facilitators may comment that men are looking for situations that make them feel sick to think about. Instruct men to work alone, and let them know that **they do not need to share what they write down with anyone**. Have men fold their papers, and then regroup for a discussion.

Discussion

Ask men, "What was it like to think about that experience? How did you feel?" Note that some men may feel overwhelmed and have already stopped thinking about their shameful behavior. Point out that it is hard to talk about shame issues and, therefore, others don't know how badly we feel about ourselves. Too much shame is debilitating and harmful.

Ask men if anyone is willing to share their experience doing this exercise with the group. If men are willing to share their experience, facilitators should support the wrongness of their actions, but then point out examples of times that this man has behaved in a different way. The purpose of this is to try to model feeling guilt rather than feeling shame. If no one is willing to disclose, discuss with men the reasons that they feel reluctant to share. Make links between men's feeling and the feelings of shame that their children likely feel about this same situation.

End this exercise by concluding that although it is hard to revisit those moments that made us feel like terrible parents, when we hold shameful experiences inside, they get bigger and more powerful. Talking about them helps lessen feelings of shame and isolation. Talking also helps in making plans to change.

PROCESS NOTES:

It is critically important for facilitators to remember the rationale for this exercise - to translate men's feelings of shame to feelings of guilt. In doing this exercise, men are put in a very vulnerable position - they are revealing what they see as shameful secrets about themselves. If facilitators react to men's descriptions with negativity, men are likely to become overwhelmed with even greater negative feelings. To avoid increasing men's shame, facilitators need to help men go as deep as possible in their shame and then counter with positive parenting examples. For example, in a past group, a man talked about his shame at repeatedly hitting his children's mother while his child watched. He reported remembering his child's look when she screamed at him to stop. Facilitators first pushed for greater depth in negative emotion by having the client reveal that he did not stop hitting his partner, even knowing how upsetting it was to his children. Then they gave examples from his discussion in past groups of times that he did change his behavior as a result of feedback from his children. These interventions allowed facilitators to emphasize that although he did something very wrong that night, recently he has been parenting differently.

It is also important to be aware of group process, and in particular, of the possibility that one of the men in the group is not participating at the same level as others. Men are likely to notice and feel uneasy with someone who is not participating. One way to handle this is to point out that for the non-sharing man, it is still not safe to be honest with the group about his behavior. Other men in the group will likely be able to identify with this distrust and provide support. Then ask men to consider how it feels to be in group with someone who is not sharing. Bring this back to the father-child relationship as a preface to the next exercise, which addresses how denial affects children. The point to make is that other men in the group are somewhat uncomfortable talking to this non-sharing man about their behavior or their feelings, just like a child would not be comfortable talking to a parent who has not been honest about his behavior. Facilitators should monitor that they are not shaming the man who has chosen not to share his actions during this discussion.

Reporting Issues

Prior to beginning this session, it is important for group facilitators to review reporting laws and to plan for how to deal with reportable instances of child maltreatment in this group. Some groups may wish to remind men about reporting requirements prior to the discussion of the behaviors that they have written about. Alternatively, facilitators may counsel openess and full honesty. If the group is being co-facilitated by leaders who are not involved in child protection, group facilitators may consider calling their local child protection services to advise them of the exercise and to get consultation on a reporting strategy.

Shameful Incidents of Abuse may Involve Children's Mothers

For men who have primarily abused their children's mother, examples of shameful situations should involve instances where they were abusive and their children were witnesses to, or aware of, this abusive behavior. The purpose and nature of this exercise is the same regardless of whether men are discussing abuse of their children or abuse of their children's mother.

Option 2: Go to exercise 2

If the facilitators decide that individual shame work is not appropriate for the group they should move directly to exercise 2.

Exercise 2: Effect of Denial on Children (10 to 20 min)

Make a transition to this short exercise on the impact of denial on children. If the group has been working through the shame exercise, facilitators can ask men to brainstorm a list of all potential effects of their denial and secrecy about their shameful behavior on their children. If the group is starting with this exercise, facilitators can draw from one man's Problem-Solving for Parents example. Included on this list should be that, when fathers deny their abusive behavior, children may:

* Blame themselves and feel they deserve to be abused
* Be angry and distance themselves
* Avoid talking to anyone about what has happened (this is a problem for children because they are too young to manage this on their own)
* Learn to distrust themselves if they are told contradictory reports of what happened
* Feel ashamed and worthless
* Make up an incorrect reason for what happened
* Learn to deny and not talk about their own feelings
* Feel lonely and isolated from their friends
* Develop unrealistic beliefs about the causes of violence

Send the message to fathers that it is lot scarier for kids when no one talks to them in an appropriate way about the abuse they have experienced or witnessed. If the child to parent-centered continuum is posted on the group walls, ensure that minimizing and denial are included as parent-centered behaviors.

Effect of Denial on Children's Mothers

If there are a number of men in the group who have been abusive towards their children's mothers, it may be useful to expand this exercise to involve a brainstorm of effects of denial on children's mothers.

Exercise 3: Problem Solving for Parents (20 to 60 min)

Continue to review men's Problem Solving for Parents homework. If possible, have a man in mind who may be ready to present an example of his personal problem-solving in a situation where his feelings of shame led to denial or minimization with his children. An example may be avoiding discussion of abuse of children's mother, or blaming a child for discipline that a father felt was too harsh (and was ashamed of). Invite men to share their homework examples with the group.

Situation:

Intention:

Is this intention about child needs or parent needs?:

Thoughts, feelings, and actions:

Effects on child:

Alternatives:

If Time, Men Evaluate their Progress

As a follow-up to problem-solving, facilitators may ask men to evaluate their own progress in using the Problem Solving for Parents steps. Ask men the questions:

> Has working through problems in this way helped you to change your thoughts?

> Has working through problems in this way helped you to change your behaviors?

> What progress do you think you are making in being more child-centered? In being less parent-centered?

> What do you think you still need to work on?

Homework (10 min)

For homework this week, men are asked to think about the session. Ask men to pay attention to whether they feel "heavier" or "lighter" during the week. Men are also asked to continue to keep the fathering log.

GOAL 4:

Consolidating learning, rebuilding trust, and planning for the future

General Notes

Goal 4: Consolidating learning, rebuilding trust, and planning for the future

The final therapeutic goal of *Caring Dads* is to consolidate learning, talk about ways that fathers can rebuild trust with their families, and plan for the future. This goal necessitates a balance between a message of hopefulness that men have taken the first steps to improved relationships with their children and appropriate caution about maintaining change over time. The process of change is an ongoing one that requires vigilance to avoid old patterns of thinking and behaving. In addition, typical concerns about termination must be addressed. We have found that many of the *Caring Dads* clients are greatly saddened by the end of the program (somewhat paradoxically, given their initial resistance to intervention). For many of our clients, the group has provided an unprecedented opportunity for them to share ideas and talk about emotional matters in a supportive and respectful environment.

Key therapeutic skills for this section include:

1. Continued distinction between guilt and shame

Many of the men who attend *Caring Dads* experience feelings of shame and guilt in relation to past behavior towards their children. By working to shift clients from feelings of shame to guilt, the hope is that men will be able to better tolerate their negative feelings and use them productively to change their future behavior. The facilitators' role in this intervention is to support clients' responsibility-taking (i.e., self-blame and guilt) for abusive actions, while at the same time, countering clients' tendencies to generalize this guilt to a pervasive sense of self-shame and worthlessness.

2. Termination work

Despite the initial reluctance of many of the clients in *Caring Dads*, our experience has been that men are often saddened by the end of group. Typical termination dynamics may be heightened by two factors. First, many of the clients have had significant, multiple experiences of abandonment. Second, many of the clients have extremely limited social support networks. The opportunity to model an appropriate and respectful ending to a relationship is an important part of the closing sessions. Facilitators should explicitly address the impending end of group and the possibility than men may have mixed feelings about saying goodbye to other group members and facilitators. It is also important to underscore that any changes that men have achieved are theirs and will travel with them (i.e., any progress is not because of the group, but because of what men have done with information from the group). Shifting the locus of control to the clients with respect to any progress they have made is an important piece of termination. Conveying hopefulness about fathers' capacity to improve their relationships with their children is also helpful.

3. Increasing men's awareness of other sources of support and supporting help-seeking norms

Improving parent-child relationships is often a long-term project. As such, it is important for men to be aware of other sources of both formal and informal support for their parenting. These sessions offer facilitators the opportunity to provide men with information about other local parenting programs. Facilitators may wish to invite representatives from other community programs to address the group. Any initiative by men to seek other services or statements that recognize the importance of support should be reinforced and praised. The idea that all parents require support and that seeking help is smart (not weak) should be an undercurrent in the final sessions of the program.

Session 15: Rebuilding Trust And Healing

Goal: Consolidating learning, rebuilding trust, and planning for the future

Exercises and Handouts	Content of Exercise
Check-in and Review (40 min)	Invite men to check in with a report on their progress in changing their parenting. If shame was the focus of last session, remind men that the purpose of the discussion was not to make them feel badly, but to help men recognize and counter shame so that they can make different choices in the future.
Exercise 1: Taking Responsibility for the Past and Moving into the Future (20 min)	Review the rationale for talking with children about past abuse. Brainstorm a list of things that fathers might say to their children about past abuse. Have men work in pairs to role play a potential discussion with their child.
Exercise 2: Rebuilding Trust (30 min)	Briefly brainstorm ways to rebuild trust that do not involve direct communication with children about the abuse. The list should include continued improvement of fathering using other resources in the community. Ask men to reflect on how long it may take to rebuild trust with their children and to speculate on how they will know when their children have begun to trust them more.
Homework (20 min)	Remind men that the end of group is approaching. Invite men to share any thoughts that they might have about this. Consider individualized post-group planning. For homework, have men identify two problems that remain in their relationships and strategies they may have learned to cope with these difficulties in more child-centered ways.

Session 15: Rebuilding Trust And Healing

Consolidating learning, rebuilding trust, and planning for the future

Theme: This session focuses on helping men plan for the future. The overall goal is to help men consider what is needed to rebuild their children's trust in them and to help their children heal. Men also begin to consider follow-up steps that they may take to become even better parents. A role-played discussion with children about past abusive behavior helps men practice the skills for communicating and taking full responsibility for their behavior. Facilitators also introduce men to the idea of additional intervention for themselves or for their children. Facilitators should be ready with specific suggestions of resources available in the community.

Materials Required for Session 15

- Worksheet: Talking to Children about Violence

Check-in and Review of Homework (40 min)

Have men check in with a report of their week. Again be sure to follow-up with men on issues that arose in their Problem-Solving for Parents exercise.

If shame was the focus of last week's session, reiterate the distinction between shame and guilt. Remind men that the purpose of the exercise completed last session was not to make men feel ashamed of their behavior: rather, it was to help them think back to a difficult time and work through it so that they can better examine and prevent such behavior in the future. Assert again that when we can recognize, reflect on, and take responsibility for our past behavior, we can work more successfully towards change.

> ### PROCESS NOTES:
>
> *Last session, men were placed in a vulnerable situation in group. For some men, this was likely a helpful exercise. Others may have felt overly vulnerable either during group or in retrospect. For this reason, it is critical that facilitators begin with a review and discussion of the exercises completed in the last session. Facilitators should respond nondefensively to men's comments or concerns about the group, while at the same time asserting the need for men to be able to face their shame.*

Exercise 1: Taking Responsibility for the Past and Moving into the Future (20 min) *adapted from the Here to Help Program

Tell men that it is best to be honest when talking with their children about past abuse and parent-centered choices. Fathers must not deny their use of parent-centered strategies or use blaming or minimizing statements when discussing their abusive actions, nor should men justify their actions. Have men quickly review examples of kinds of statements that justify or blame others for bad parenting choices. Examples include: blaming the child, blaming the child's mother, dismissing the incident, emphasizing that the incident was "not all that bad", etc.

Brainstorm a list of healthy statements that fathers might make to their children about past abuse. The list of statements should include child-focused comments such as:

- It's not your fault
- I will listen to you
- I am sorry that you saw/heard my violence. What I did was not OK
- I am sorry that I did something that made you feel worried, hurt, or unsafe
- There is nothing you could have done to prevent/change what happened
- You can tell me how you feel. How you feel is important
- We can talk about what to do to keep you feeling safe it if ever happens again
- What happened was not okay - I should not have done what I did
- It must have been scary for you

Initiate a discussion with men about having conversations with children about their abuse. Ask if any of the men in group have already spoken to their children about their abusive and parent-centered actions. If so, ask men to share with the group how the conversations went. Facilitators should emphasize the courage needed to have a conversation like this with children. Ask men to speculate on whether they can cope with their children saying "Dad, you did a bad thing." Emphasize that in a discussion like this, the most important thing that men can do is listen to their children and understand their children's experience. Also make the point that it is very important for men to not become defensive and begin to deny or minimize their children's experiences or blame others for their behavior. This information is summarized for men on the Talking to Children about Violence worksheet.

Have men work in pairs to role play a discussion with their child about past abuse. Facilitators may wish to begin this process by modeling a role-played conversation or by having a man volunteer to role play his discussion in front of the group. Then, men can be placed in pairs to practice having this type of conversation. If possible, pair men who have begun these conversations with their children with men who have not yet had these discussions.

PROCESS NOTES:

Facilitators should be prepared for the question: "What if children do not want to hear about it?" It is important for facilitators to acknowledge that children sometimes do not want to talk about, or hear about, past abuse. Fathers will appreciate that, just as it may be difficult for them to talk about abuse, it is also difficult and scary for children to talk about it. Let men know that they can provide the opening for this discussion (e.g., "I wanted to let you know that I realize that when I ____ I did something wrong and that it must have been very scary for you. Do you want to talk about that time?"). However, fathers must be patient and responsive to children's needs, and not badger children to have a conversation they may not yet feel safe to have. Fathers can always try to discuss it at another time, or simply be ready to talk when children bring up these issues. It can be helpful for children to hear that the father will be ready to listen if the child wants to talk about it at another time. Other opportunities to watch for are times when children may be worried that a pattern from the past will repeat itself (e.g., when a child flinches or expresses anger or distrust in the father's actions).

Facilitators should also be ready to address men's concerns that they will not be able to handle talking to their children about violence or abuse - that such conversations will open up too many areas of discussion and they will not know how to handle the situation. In response to these types of comments, it is good for facilitators to emphasize these things:

- *That the most important part of the process is fathers' willingness to listen and empathize with their children's experience*
- *That fathers are the adults in the relationship, and even though it is difficult, fathers may need to listen to their children express disappointment or anger with them*
- *That men are best to fall back on the basics of accountability in responding to unexpected comments from their children*
- *That fathers can seek help in undertaking this conversation*

Exercise 2: Rebuilding Trust (30 min)

Let men know that communicating with children is an important way to rebuild trust. However, there are also other things that man can do. Encourage men to brainstorm other ways to rebuild trust. The list should include:

- Providing a predictable and safe environment
- Being consistent in moods and behaviors
- Continuing to work to improve their fathering
- Responding to children's needs
- Showing positive attention
- Nurturing children
- Providing activities that children can enjoy and be successful at
- Maintaining respective behavior towards people that are important to children, especially their mothers

In general, facilitators wish to leave men with a message of hope. Emphasize that if men are able to take responsibility for the past and maintain non-abusive behavior in the present, then their children will most likely come to trust them again. Facilitators may follow-up on this statement by asking men to share examples of indications that they have already stated to rebuild trust with their children.

Facilitators should also emphasize that children and/or families sometimes need help from other professionals, like child therapists or women's advocates, to improve things in their family. Fathers are sometimes reluctant to see their family members involved in therapy for fear that it will make the situation worse. Return to the idea of parent needs and child needs and have men consider whether their need to keep things secret, or their distrust of a system, is preventing them from seeking services that will benefit their children or family. Provide examples of services in the community that men could turn to for help. (Help-seeking will be discussed in the final session as well).

> **PROCESS NOTES:**
>
> *Facilitators should be sure to let men know that children tend to react to changes, even positive ones, with more difficult behavior (e.g., with difficulty sleeping, eating, higher levels of noncompliance). This is especially the case when children have experienced abuse. When children are still worried about abuse occurring, they often do not show these feelings at home. Instead, their anger, anxiety, and hurt may show in aggressive or unmotivated behavior at school, or in physical symptoms, such as stomach aches or difficulties sleeping. Once children feel safer, they may begin expressing these feelings more directly in angry or hurt words or behaviors. Let fathers know that their reactions are normal, and can be signs of progress. Help them to appreciate that to support the healing process, it is very important that they maintain child-centered parenting in spite of their children's angry or difficult behaviors.*

Responding to Concerns About Mothers Influence

Men are sometimes concerned that their partners have poisoned their children against them. If this issue arises in discussion, first remind men of the need to focus their attention away from their anger at their partner and towards their interaction with their children. Then, have men come up with examples of how they can influence their children's perception of them as a father, regardless of the opinions of others. Assert that children will ultimately make their own decisions about their fathers.

Homework (20 min)

Before assigning homework, remind men that the end of group is approaching and invite them to share any thoughts about group termination. Facilitators should be ready to check in with men about individualized post-group intervention planning. Planning is particularly critical for those men who facilitators feel should be engaged in another intervention service by the time that *Caring Dads* has ended. Depending on the needs of men in the group, facilitators may wish to end the group ten minutes early so that these individual meetings can occur during group time. Alternatively, they can invite men to remain after group.

For homework, have men identify the one or two problems that remain for them, and one or two strategies that they have learned for coping with these difficulties in a more child-centered manner. For men whose primary difficulty is relating to children's mothers modifications can be made in the homework assignment so that men are identifying continued difficulties in and coping strategies for their relationship with children's mothers.

Session 16: What About Discipline?

Goal: Consolidating learning, rebuilding trust, and planning for the future

Exercises and Handouts	Content of Exercise
Check-in (30 min)	Have men check in with a review of their homework.
Exercise 1: Summarizing Alternatives to Abusive and Parent-Centered Behaviors (50 minutes)	Remind men that over the past few weeks, they have generated a list of child-centered alternatives for difficult parenting situations. Facilitators should hand out a transcribed list for men to review. Present men with the following child management options and categorize each of the strategies on the transcribed list. 1. Changing parental demands 2. Arranging the situation so that this argument doesn't come up 3. Encouraging/supporting child's positive behaviors 4. Using natural consequences 5. Understanding and meeting the child's underlying need
Exercise 2: Defining Discipline (20 minutes)	Present a definition of discipline. Review behaviors from men's list that do not fall into the above list of strategies. Are these examples of discipline? Where possible, have men role play the application of these strategies to the difficult situations that they identified as part of their homework.
Homework (10 min)	In the second week of *Caring Dads*, men identified hopes and goals for developing better relationships with their children. For homework this week, have men review these goals and identify progress they have made towards meeting them.

Session 16: What About Discipline?

Goal: Consolidating learning, rebuilding trust and planning for the future

Theme: To rebuild trust in the father-child relationship, it is important that fathers maintain child-centered parenting and avoid abuse, even in the face of child misbehavior. So far, information on alternative strategies for managing child misbehavior has been embedded in lessons around men's problem-solving. This session is devoted to bringing these lessons together to provide men with a set of options for dealing with child misbehavior. Facilitators should continue to emphasize the need for men to examine their behavior and for them to rely on child-centered parenting strategies.

Materials Required for Session 16

- Transcribed list of alternatives generated in past sessions

- Worksheet: Alternative methods of child management

RATIONALE FOR FACILITATORS

One of the most difficult aspects of running Caring Dads groups is the lack of ability to fix problems in men's families. Many of the men who come to group are facing a large number of parenting issues and general life stressors. They often come to group each week with a new crisis or issue in their family. We operate with the assumption that men's reactive and punitive behaviors have been significant contributors to these crises. Thus, rather than deal with the crisis or behavior management issues as they arise, we spend time attempting to alter the patterns of fathers' reactions and behaviors. Sometimes this strategy of intervention seems to have an immediate and observable impact. For example, one of the fathers in Caring Dads complained that his six-year-old was consistently noncompliant. After the early sessions on child-centered parenting, this father decided to spend a half hour each night playing with his young child. The result was a significant decrease in his child's behavior problems and noncompliance. As another example, a father was worried that his teenage son was avoiding access visits and pulling away from him. He found that when he committed to ending complaints about this child's mother, and instead focused on getting to know his son better, his son stopped avoiding visits.

For other men, issues continue to arise even when fathers appear to engage in relatively child-centered parenting. In many cases, these are fathers who are in prolonged and hostile custody and access battles, who are co-parenting with very unhealthy and distressed mothers, or who have children with physical or behavioral conditions that are difficult for any parent to manage. In these cases, focusing on helping fathers be less reactive and more child-centered will not solve all the issues in the family. However, if men are able to maintain such behavior, it will provide a necessary safe haven for children. Moreover, a positive experience in the Caring Dads group will be a springboard for men to become involved in additional services appropriate to the needs of their children and families.

The current session on managing child misbehavior should be facilitated with the above rationale in mind. Specific strategies of child management are suggested, but all should be presented in the context of the need for the use of Problem-Solving for Parents steps. The continued need for men to understand and appreciate their children and to use child-centered parenting remains paramount.

Check-in (30 min)

Have men check in with a review of their homework (i.e., identification of remaining problems with children). Facilitators should make a list of issues around child management on the flip-chart as they arise.

Exercise 1: Summarizing Alternatives to Abusive and Parent-Centered Behaviors (50 min)

Remind men that over the past sessions, the group has generated a list of alternatives to abusive and parent-centered behaviors. Explain that during this session, the group will return to this list and talk more about alternative ways to manage child misbehavior that will avoid abuse and allow rebuilding of trust.

Give men the transcribed list of alternatives to punishment that facilitators compiled on the basis of men's responses to the last question of the Problem Solving for Parents exercises. Have men review this list.

Introduce men to five categories of strategies to respond to child misbehavior and explain each of them. Refer men to the Alternative Methods of Child Management worksheet.

1. Changing parental demands

2. Arranging the situation so that the argument doesn't come up

3. Encouraging/supporting children's positive behaviors

4. Using natural consequences

5. Understanding and meeting children's underlying needs

Have men solidify their knowledge by classifying each of the alternatives listed on their handouts into one of these five categories of child management strategies. Also make a list of alternatives that do not fit into any of the above categories.

Next, invite one of the men in group to share his child management situation and to apply this set of problem-solving strategies to his situation. Have the group work though the application of each of the five strategies of managing child misbehavior. The following example refers to a parent dealing with the challenge of a child not completing homework:

Example: Application of parenting strategies to a child who is not completing her homework.

1. Changing Parental Demands. I can change my demands. I may be able to allow her to avoid her homework tonight. I could request that she do some, but not all, of her homework. I can simply ask that she turn off the television and then hope that she will do her homework.

2. Arrange the situation so that this argument doesn't come up. I could have a discussion with her about homework in general. I could reflect that it is difficult to do homework this late at night. We can make a plan that homework will always be done at a certain time. We can also make a plan for what I should do if she forgets about her homework. We can decide if I should remind her and how I should remind her.

3. Encourage/support the child's positive behaviors. I could offer to help her with her homework. I could make sure that she knows I am interested in what she is learning at school. I could supplement her education with something at home.

4. Using natural consequences or outside authorities. Instead of getting mad at her, can I encourage her to do her homework and then support the school's consequences if it is not finished?

5. Meeting the child's underlying need. What is my daughter's misbehavior really about? She usually completes her homework, so something may be different tonight. Is she upset, tired, angry, or frustrated tonight? I can listen carefully to what she says about her day to try to figure this out.

PROCESS NOTES:

It is sometimes difficult for men to accept that these strategies can be as successful as more intimidating and parent-centered actions. Facilitators should acknowledge that parent-centered and abusive methods often lead to immediate compliance, but that there are significant negative long-term consequences with these forms of parenting. Thus, in the longer-term, these strategies will not be successful. In explaining this, it is sometimes helpful to use the analogy of fixing a car - when you fix it using a stop-gap measure, the car ends up having more problems and costing more money in the long run.

Children may not be ready to comply with requests

Facilitators need to remember that because men have been abusive towards their children, it will likely take a long time before their children will comply readily with requests, especially more difficult requests. Thus, facilitators should be vigilant to helping men make modest plans for child management and should model the idea of taking small steps towards bigger changes.

Exercise 2: Defining Discipline (20 min)

In the following exercise, men are asked to brainstorm differences between discipline and parent-centered or abusive behaviors. This exercise acts as a review of the definition of abuse and sets men up for a more in-depth discussion of discipline.

Facilitators should ensure that the following definitions are derived:

Discipline or child-centered managment refers to parental actions that teach a child more appropriate behaviors and helps a child develop self-control strategies.

- Purpose is to teach/help children learn appropriate behaviors, good habits (not simply to control the child)
- Teaches children a specific behavior for their own benefit, rather than for the parent's benefit
- Is developmentally appropriate
- Follows logically from the offending behavior
- Is consistently applied
- Helps the child grow into an independent individual with a sense of self-worth
- Child feels guilty, but not ashamed. Thus, the child feels confident that he or she will be able to do things differently in the future

Abusive and/or parent-centered actions

- Purpose is to make the child pay
- Is about getting the child in trouble rather than helping him/her learn
- Child learns to avoid behavior out of fear, not for any other reason (safety, morality, best interests etc.)
- Child doesn't learn alternate ways to resolve problem or control behavior
- Diminishes self-esteem, self-respect, and respect for others
- Is disproportionate to the child's behavior

Facilitators should stress the differences in method and outcomes of abuse and discipline. Emphasize that if men use discipline, they will provide their children with a basis to make a good choice for themselves. This foundation remains even if the father is not there so that children can be trusted to make good decisions when their parents are not around.

Have men go back to the list of alternatives that they generated. Are any of the remaining examples discipline?

It is useful to consolidate learning in one of two ways. In small groups, facilitators can review men's difficult child management situations and work towards generating alternatives that fall under each of the five listed strategies. They may also review the methods men suggested for dealing with these situations and reflect on whether men are using discipline or parent-centered actions.

Alternatively, men can be instructed to role play the use of various child management strategies. In this case, role plays are best done by having men: 1) identify the situation; 2) decide on a strategy; 3) determine what and how this strategy should be implemented; and then 4) role play its implementation. For example, if a father decided to handle the homework situation by making a general plan for when homework is completed (see example), men can role play this conversation.

Different Definitions of Discipline

We have used the term discipline to refer to child-centered methods of teaching children how to manage themselves in the world. For some of the men in our groups, the word discipline is strongly associated with a very rigid, strict and severe style of parenting - not with the more child-centered meaning that we are trying to convey. If men in the group define discipline in this more negative way, facilitators should feel free to refer to these parenting behaviors simply as "child-centered child management".

Homework (10 min)

For homework this session, men are asked to begin to consider what they have learned, and what has changed for them, as a result of attending this program. In the second week of *Caring Dads*, men identified hopes and goals for developing better relationships with their children. For homework this week, men are also asked to review these hopes and goals and identify progress they have made towards meeting them.

Session 17: Wrapping Up

Goal: Consolidating learning, rebuilding trust, and planning for the future

Exercises and Handouts	Content of Exercise
Check-in and Homework Review (25 minutes)	Have men reflect on one thing that they have learned over the past 16 weeks. Encourage comments and feedback from other group members.
Exercise 1: Review of Main Concepts (40 minutes)	Ask men to brainstorm a list of concepts that they learned over the past 16 weeks. Be sure the following are included: · the parent-centered to child-centered continuum · the thoughts, feelings, action triangle · listening to, praising, and nurturing children · developmental stages · the definition of child abuse · the Problem-Solving for Parents steps · talking with children about past abuse · alternative ways to manage problems with children
Exercise 2: Where am I Going From Here? (20 minutes)	Discuss resources available in the community for parents. Also, talk to men about informal sources of parenting support. Men should brainstorm a list of informal resources they could use for additional parenting support after the end of group.
Exercise 3: Feedback for the Group (15 minutes)	Invite men to offer suggestions for future groups.
Checkout (10 minutes)	Invite each man to check out with his thoughts about group.

Session 17: Wrapping Up

Consolidating learning, rebuilding trust, and planning for the future

Theme: In this last session, men should be encouraged to reflect on what they have learned at *Caring Dads*, on changes that they have made over the course of group, and on their plans for the future. Facilitators should emphasize the need for men to continually work towards improving their fathering, and to be ready to seek additional support as their children enter different developmental stages. Because this is the final week, facilitators may also wish to celebrate the end of group in a more informal manner. Some groups, for example, have decided to have pizza together during this last session.

Materials Required for Session 17

- List of parenting resources available in the community and/or pamphlets for these programs

Check-in and Homework Review (25 min)

Have men check in by reflecting on changes that they have made over the course of the group. Encourage group discussion.

> **PROCESS NOTES:**
>
> *Without feedback, men seldom appreciate how angry or closed they were at the beginning of group. This appreciation is important for helping men consider how they might approach help-providers in the future. With this in mind, facilitators may consider encouraging other group members to share their memories of other men in the group from the first few weeks. However, facilitators also need to ensure that this discussion induces hope about change rather then shame about past behavior.*
>
> *It is useful for facilitators to remember that group termination is often difficult. Clients of Caring Dads sometimes comment that this group was the first time that they felt that their thoughts and feelings were heard and respected by the "system." In the face of termination, men present in a variety of ways. Sometimes, men who have been generally good participants in group will stop participating or become argumentative. Other times, men will come to group with a continued list of crises that need immediate group attention. Still other men will appear to detach from group. Facilitators should remember that these reactions may relate to termination and should respond with appropriate levels of empathy and curiosity about men's thoughts and feelings around ending group.*

Review some of the concepts and ideas discussed over the past 16 weeks. This review provides a chance to consolidate and underscore all of the work men have done over the course of *Caring Dads*. Have men brainstorm a list of concepts/exercises/ideas that they remember. Make the review as interactive as possible, calling on men to provide examples of the different concepts from their experiences with their children and families. Facilitators should also ensure that the following concepts are covered during the review:

Parent-centered to child-centered continuum

When parenting, men are constantly making choices to balance meeting their own needs and the needs of their children. The *Caring Dads* group has encouraged men to make their children's needs a higher priority. The group also discussed how parents who consistently choose to meet parent needs and ignore child needs are being abusive to their children.

Listening to, praising, and nurturing children

Men learned that key building blocks to a good relationship with children are listening, praising and nurturing. Have men review each of these concepts. Also emphasize that, without listening, men are likely to misunderstand or be unaware of their children's needs.

Developmental stages

Children are not small adults. As they get older, children differ in their thinking, their ability to manage emotions and behavior, their needs and their understanding of sexuality. To appreciate why a child may be acting in a certain way, it is important to understand their developmental strengths and limitations.

Thoughts, feelings, action triangle

Men learned that there are thoughts and feelings connected to every action and that to understand why we behave the way we do, it is useful to figure out how we are feeling and what we are thinking. Men were also taught that the most effective way to change their behavior is to change their thoughts.

Definition of child abuse

In *Caring Dads*, child abuse is broadly defined as those behaviors that are harmful to children's physical and emotional well-being. Abusive behaviors include a wide range of actions that fall at the parent-centered end of the parenting continuum. Fathers also need to understand that the official definition of child abuse is much narrower than the one used in the *Caring Dads* group.

Problem-solving for parents

Men were given a set of steps to work through when faced with difficult parenting situations. These steps include: identifying the situation; considering child and adult needs; using the thinking, feeling, action triangle, considering the impact of actions taken, and generating alternative actions. Men are encouraged to continue using these problem-solving steps.

Talking with children about past abuse

Remind men that to rebuild trust, it is important to be honest with children about past abuse and parent-centered behavior.

Alternative ways to manage problems with children

Finally, review the material covered in the last session on alternative ways to manage problems with children. Because this material is new to men, it is likely useful to have them brainstorm the entire list of alternative methods (i.e., change parental demands, arrange the situation so that this argument doesn't come up, encourage/support child's positive behaviors, use natural consequences, understand and meet the child's underlying need, and use appropriate discipline to help teach the child).

Exercise 2: Where am I Going From Here? (20 min)

Facilitators should use this opportunity to share with men ideas about how to get support for their parenting once the group has ended. Facilitators can present a list of formal resources available in their community. Review each resource and discuss the nature of the service and the cost to the participant. Having pamphlets available from other programs can also be helpful. Facilitators should be aware that many communities have free or low-cost parenting programs offered by public health. Other more specialized language and culture-specific programs should also be reviewed. If appropriate, facilitators may want to take some time in group to offer specific suggestions to men about additional intervention. As has already been emphasized, this program is not sufficient to meet the needs of all men making changes in their fathering behavior. Moreover, men often need longer-term support to maintain positive fathering of their children.

Next, ask men to talk about less formal sources of parenting support. Generally, men have not had the same experience with children as women and have less knowledge about children's basic abilities and needs. Facilitators should acknowledge that there are many, many things to know about children and that it is difficult to keep track of it all.

Men should then brainstorm actions that they could take if they are not sure if their behaviors and expectations are reasonable, or if they need some additional information/suggestions about managing a particular situation. This list should include the following suggestions:

- Ask your child at a time unrelated to any problematic behavior
- Watch your child's friends
- Ask around. Other parents and family members are good sources of this kind of information
- Go to the library or bookstore and get a book on parenting. Books often have information about what can be expected of children at different ages
- Ask a day care provider
- Ask your child's teacher
- Ask a nurse or your family doctor
- Ask other fathers

Exercise 3: Feedback for the Group (15 min)

Compliment men for taking steps to improve their relationship with their children. Let them know that the completion of this program has been an important step for them. Congratulate them on their participation and effort.

Invite men to share their feedback about the group with the facilitators and with other group members. Let men know their suggestions for improvement are valuable.

Checkout (10 min)

Have men check out with their thoughts and feelings about the end of group.

APPENDIX A:

Program Workbook

Session 2 Homework
Three Hopes I Have for My Children

Three hopes I have to improve my relationship with my child or children are:

1. _____

2. _____

3. _____

One goal I have for my relationship with my child or children is:
(This goal will be discussed in group).

1. _____

Session 3
Feelings Sheet

Affection

Loved	Wanted
Liked	Friendly towards
Adored	Warm
Appreciated	Empathetic
Concerned for	Enchanted
Cared for	Tenderness for

Dislike

Animosity	Indifferent
Wish to shun	Cold toward
Repelled by	Withdrawn
Detest	Despise

Hopeful

Anticipate	Expecting
Confident	Aspiring
Faith in	Trustful of
Keen	

Despairing

Hopeless	Desperate
Trapped	Insecure
Discouraged	Defeated
Dominated	

Happy

Joyful	Satisfied
Calm	Delighted
Pleased	Surprised
Contented	Fulfilled
Proud	Serene
Comfortable	Happy
Supported	Completed
Elated	Grateful
Alive	Peaceful

Unhappy

Ashamed	Grieved
Sad	Lonely
Embarrassed	Guilty
Depressed	Put-down
Cheated	Remorseful
Rejected	Sinful
Hurt	Humiliated
Sorry	Sorrowful
Upset	Dissatisfied

Courageous

Risky	Daring
Brave	Confident
Bold	Enduring
Gusty	Determined
Valiant	

Fearful or Nervous

Afraid	Cowardly
Cautious	Scared
Up-tight	Startled
Terrified	Distrustful
Trapped	Nervous
Anxious	Apprehensive
Edgy	Tense
	Worried

Proud or Capable

Admired	Worthy
Awed	Respected
Important	Esteemed
Approved of	Independent
Strong	Confident
Secure	Smart

Mad

Angry	Infuriated
Bored	Provoked
Indignant	Disdainful
Hurt	Contemptuous
Furious	Annoyed
Antagonistic	

Excited

Vibrant	Eager
Zealous	Optimistic
Enthusiastic	Interested

Confused

Puzzled
Mixed up
Dismayed

Session 3: Fathering Circles Past

What My Father Felt Like

This circle represents your feelings as a child. We would like you to think about what it felt like to be parented by your father and all of the feelings you had for your father. Label them on the circle. Remember, the size of the section you label should represent the size of the feeling. For example, if fear was your biggest feeling, then it should have the biggest section. Again, feel free to use words that are not on the sheet.

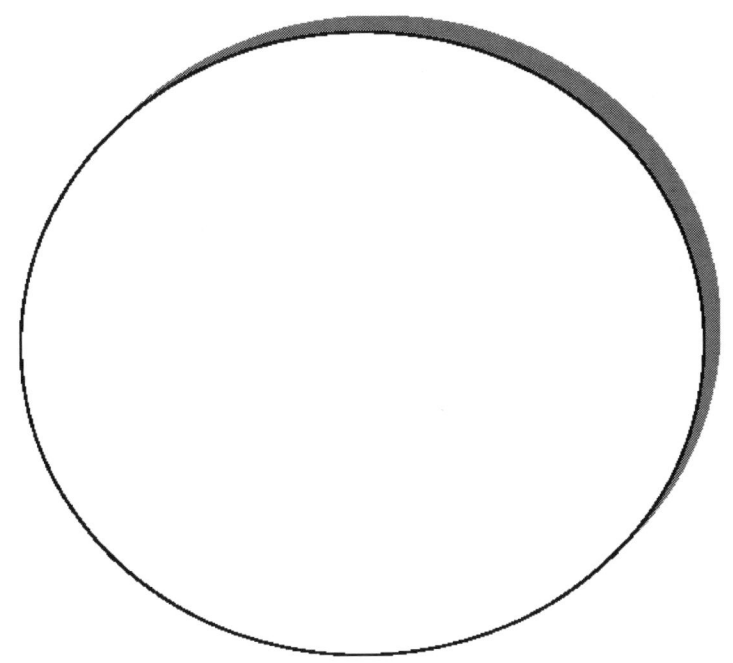

As a child I felt _____ towards my father.

Admiration	Fear	Pride
Blame	Happiness	Respect
Guilt	Hate	Shame
Caring	Contentment	Trust
Disgust	Love	Sadness

Session 3: Fathering Circles Present

How I Think My Child Feels

With this sheet you are again identifying feelings from a child's perspective. This time, instead of identifying your feelings toward your own father when you were a child, you are to complete the circle first with how you think your child feels about you.

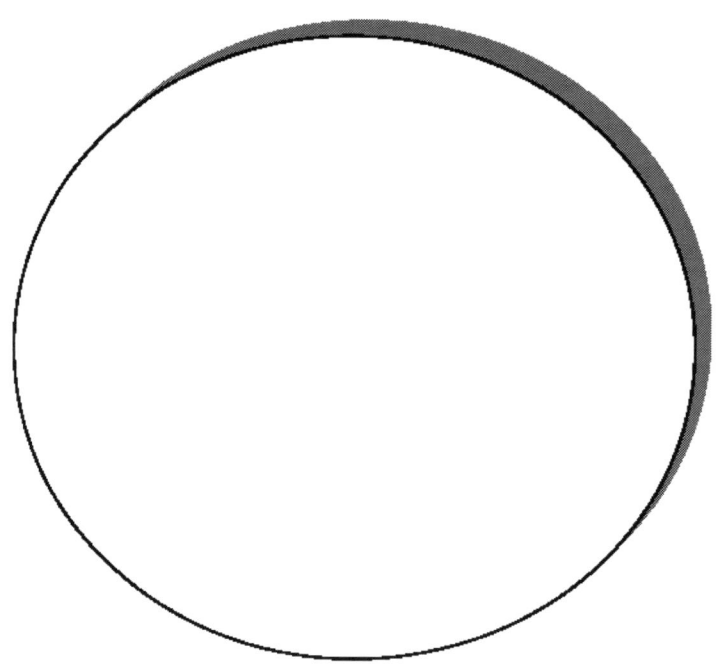

I think that my child feels _____ towards me.

Admiration	Fear	Pride
Blame	Happiness	Respect
Guilt	Hate	Shame
Caring	Contentment	Trust
Disgust	Love	Sadness

Session 3: Fathering Circles Ideal

How I Would Like My Child to Feel About Me

The circle below represents the way you would like your child to feel towards you. At the bottom of page is a list of feelings a child may have towards his or her father. Your job is to divide up the circle below and label it to represent the way you would like your child to feel about you. For example, if you would like your child to feel a bit of admiration for you, you could fill in a bit of the circle with admiration.

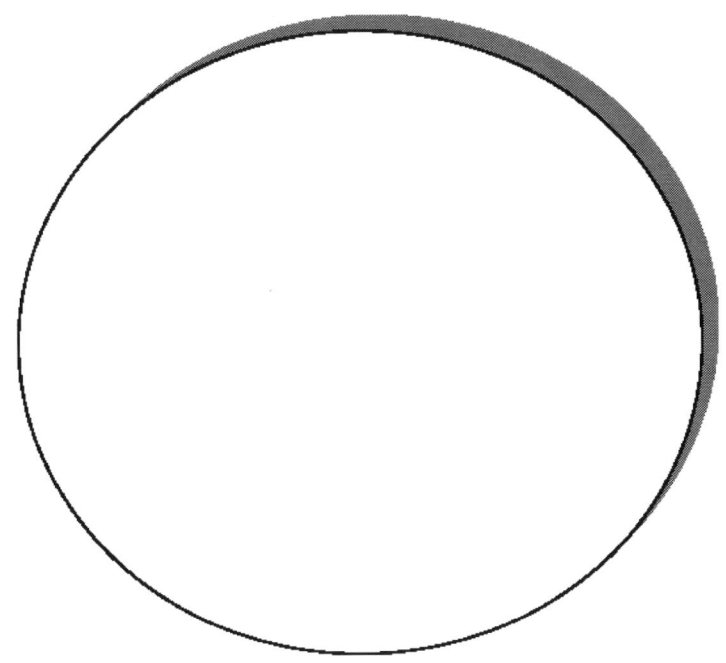

I would like my child to feel _____ towards me.

Admiration	Fear	Pride
Blame	Happiness	Respect
Guilt	Hate	Shame
Caring	Contentment	Trust
Disgust	Love	Sadness

Session 3 Homework

Weekly Fathering Log

Name: _____ Week of: _____

This week, things I felt good about as a father were:

_____

_____

_____

Three ways that I praised my child this week:
(Be as specific as possible. What did you say?)

_____

_____

_____

_____

_____

This week, things I struggled with as a father were:

_____

_____

_____

_____

_____

If I were to rate how I felt about my parenting this past week on a scale of 1-5, where 1 means I did not feel good at all about the parenting choices I made and 5 means I felt great, my week was:

_____

Session 4
Nurturing Wheel

LOVE AND CARE FOR YOUR CHILDREN

TRUST AND RESPECT
Acknowledge children's right to have own feelings, friends, activities and opinions • Promote independence • Allow for privacy • Respect feelings for other parent • Believe your children.

PROMOTE EMOTIONAL SECURITY
Talk and act so that children feel safe and comfortable expressing themselves • Be gentle • Be dependable.

CARE FOR YOURSELF
Give yourself personal time • Keep yourself healthy • Maintain friendships • Accept love.

PROVIDE PHYSICAL SECURITY
Provide food, shelter, clothing • Teach personal hygiene and nutrition • Monitor safety • Maintain a family routine • attend to wounds.

NURTURING CHILDREN

GIVE AFFECTION
Express verbal and physical affection • Be affectionate when your children are physically or emotionally hurt.

PROVIDE DISCIPLINE
Be consistent • Ensure rules are appropriate to age and development of child • Be clear about limits and expectations • Use discipline to give instruction, not punish.

ENCOURAGE AND SUPPORT
Be affirming • Encourage children to follow their interest • Let children disagree with you • Recognize improvement • Teach new skills • Let them make mistakes.

GIVE TIME
Participate in your children's lives: activities, school, sports, special events and days, celebrations, friends • Include your children in your activities • Reveal who you are to your children.

LOVE AND CARE FOR YOUR CHILDREN

Developed by the Domestic Abuse Intervention Project, 202 East Superior St., Duluth, MN 55802

Session 4
Parenting Continuum

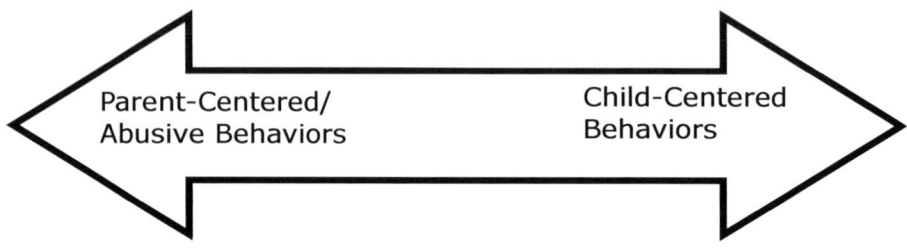

Parent-Centered/
Abusive Behaviors

Child-Centered
Behaviors

Denigrates, insults child

Expresses conditional love and
ambivalent feelings towards child

Emotionally or physically rejects
child's attention

Uses cruel & harsh control methods

Shows no sensitivity to child's
needs

Intentionally seeks out ways to
frighten, threaten or provoke
child

Responds unpredictably with
emotional discharge through
coercion, threats, or bribes

Is sexually or physically coercive
or intrusive

Provides a variety of sensory
stimulation & positive emotional expression

Engages in highly competent,
child-centered interactions

Communicates to child about
normal sexuality & healthy
relationships

Makes rules for safety and
health

Occasionally scolds, criticizes,
interrupts child activity

Session 4

When Praise is Not Really Praise at All

Sometimes we think that we are praising our child when we are not really praising him or her at all.

In **real praise**, the purpose of the "praiser" is to let the child know how pleased they are with the child, and how valued and special the child is. <u>That's all!</u>

In **unresponsive forms of praise** the child does not feel valued. The message to the child is that whatever he or she did or is not good enough.

Watch out for the following forms of "non-praise" or "unresponsive praise."

Praise is unresponsive when:

- it's not honest

- you only praise in comparison to others

- it's not consistent with the situation in nature or extent

- it's especially selective (e.g. praise only for sports or school)

- there's a "but" added on (e.g. that was great, but ....)

- you add "next time you should..."

- you add "you could do even better if..."

- praise is qualified (e.g. "for you, that was pretty good", or "for a ___, that was pretty good.")

- praise is "taken back" right afterwards "(e.g. "that's really good. When I was your age, I could do even better.")

Session 4 Homework
Weekly Fathering Log

Name: _____ Week of: _____

This week, things I felt good about as a father were:

_____

_____

_____

Three ways that I praised my child this week:

(Be as specific as possible. What did you say?)

_____

_____

_____

_____

_____

This week, things I struggled with as a father were:

_____

_____

_____

_____

_____

If I were to rate how I felt about my parenting this past week on a scale of 1-5, where 1 means I did not feel good at all about the parenting choices I made and 5 means I felt great, my week was:

_____

Session 5
How Well Do I Know My Child? - Quiz

PRESCHOOL AGE (If your child is not yet in school)

1. Provide a description of your child's physical characteristics (e.g., eye colour, hair colour, approximate height).

_____

_____

_____

2. What are your child's favourite toys?

_____

3. What is your child most interested in learning about?

_____

4. What activity can your child do for a long time without getting bored?

_____

5. What does your child most like to do with you? With his/her mother?

_____

6. What is the best way to know if your child is upset?

_____

7. What is most likely to make your child upset?

_____

8. What is your child's biggest fear?

_____

9. What is most likely to make your child happy?

_____

SCHOOL AGE

1. Provide a description of your child's physical characteristics (e.g., eye colour, hair colour, approximate height).

_____

_____

_____

2. What are your child's favourite toys and games?

_____

3. What does your child want to be when he/she grows up?

_____

4. If it was your child's birthday tomorrow, what would he/she want?

_____

5. What does your child most like to do with you? With his/her mother? With friends?

_____

6. What is the best way to know if your child is upset?

_____

7. What does your child worry about most? What is your child's biggest fear?

_____

8. What is the most recent disappointment that your child has faced?

_____

9. What does your child take most pride in?

_____

TEENAGE

1. Provide a description of your child's physical characteristics (e.g., eye colour, hair colour, approximate height).

_____

_____

_____

2. What are your child's favourite and least favourite subjects in school?

_____

3. What is your child's favourite music group?

_____

4. Who are your child's friends? What does he/she like to do with them?

_____

5. What does your child like to do with you? With his/her mother?

_____

6. Who does your child confide in when he/she is upset?

_____

7. What is the best way to know if your child is upset or worried?

_____

8. What does your child worry about most? What is your child's biggest fear?

_____

9. What is the most recent disappointment that your child has faced?

_____

10. What does your child take most pride in?

_____

Session 5 Homework
Weekly Fathering Log

Name: _____ Week of: _____

This week, things I felt good about as a father were:

_____

_____

_____

Three ways that I praised my child this week:

(Be as specific as possible. What did you say?)

_____

_____

_____

_____

_____

This week, things I struggled with as a father were:

_____

_____

_____

_____

If I were to rate how I felt about my parenting this past week on a scale of 1-5, where 1 means I did not feel good at all about the parenting choices I made and 5 means I felt great, my week was:

_____

Session 6
Tips for Being a Good Listener

1. Make time for your children

2. Pay attention

3. Resist fixing the problem

4. Ask questions

5. Figure out, talk about, and accept what your children are feeling

6. Get to know how your child likes to talk

Session 6
Relationship Building Challenges

Part 1

Look over the following relationship-building behaviors and identify those that you find challenging.

I find it challenging to:

Tell my child that I love him/her	Yes	No
Give my child my full attention when he/she wants to talk	Yes	No
Ask my child about his or her feelings	Yes	No
Help my child with his or her homework	Yes	No
Talk about my child's feelings without an argument	Yes	No
Play a game my child has chosen	Yes	No
Spend long periods of time alone with my child	Yes	No
Teach my child something new	Yes	No
Keep track of my child's schedule	Yes	No
Tell my child that he or she has done a good job	Yes	No
Apologize to my child when I am wrong	Yes	No
Support my child's relationship with his or her mother	Yes	No
Support my child's mother without conflict	Yes	No

Are there other relationship-building behaviors that you find challenging?

_____

_____

_____

Part 2

List two obstacles to engaging in these relationship-building behaviors. For each obstacle, identify things that you can do to overcome that obstacle.

Obstacle 1: _____

What I can do:

1. _____

2. _____

3. _____

Obstacle 2: _____

What I can do:

1. _____

2. _____

3. _____

Session 6 Homework
Weekly Fathering Log

Name: _____ Week of: _____

This week, things I felt good about as a father were:

_____

_____

_____

Three ways that I praised my child this week:

(Be as specific as possible. What did you say?)

_____

_____

_____

_____

_____

This week, things I struggled with as a father were:

_____

_____

_____

_____

If I were to rate how I felt about my parenting this past week on a scale of 1-5, where 1 means I did not feel good at all about the parenting choices I made and 5 means I felt great, my week was:

_____

Session 7
What Kind of Example Do I Set?

Use the following scale to rate yourself. What kind of example do you set for your child or children with the way that you treat their mother? What kind of things are they learning about relationships?

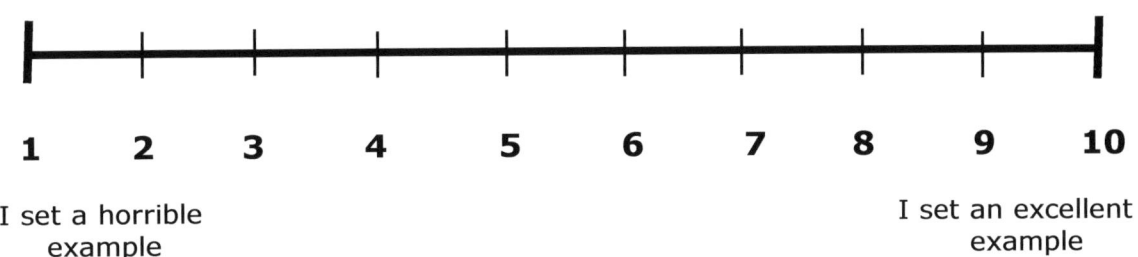

| 1 | 2 | 3 | 4 | 5 | 6 | 7 | 8 | 9 | 10 |

I set a horrible
example

I set an excellent
example

Session 7 Homework
Being a Good Model for My Children

This week, list three things that you do that provide a good example to your children. If your children have a relationship with their mother, make sure that one is an example from your relationship with her or supporting the children's relationship with her.

1. _____

2. _____

3. _____

Session 7 Homework
Weekly Fathering Log

Name: _____ Week of: _____

This week, things I felt good about as a father were:

_____

_____

_____

Three ways that I praised my child this week:

(Be as specific as possible. What did you say?)

_____

_____

_____

_____

_____

_____

This week, things I struggled with as a father were:

_____

_____

_____

_____

_____

If I were to rate how I felt about my parenting this past week on a scale of 1-5, where 1 means I did not feel good at all about the parenting choices I made and 5 means I felt great, my week was:

_____

Session 8 Worksheet
Thoughts, Feelings, Actions Triangle

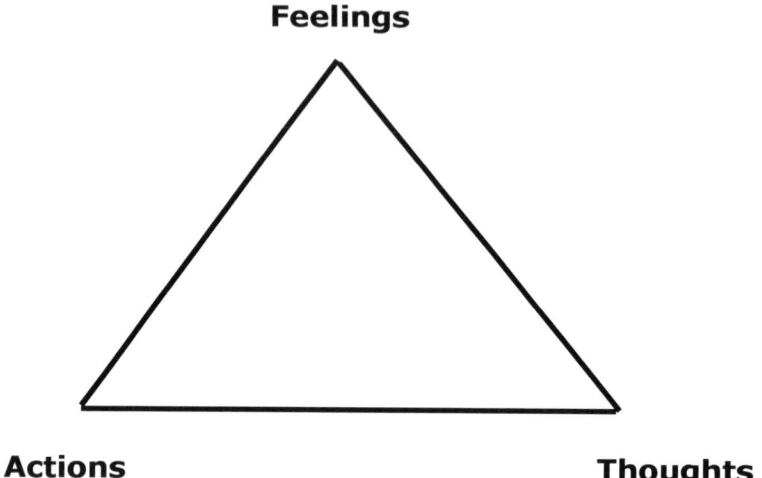

Session 8 Worksheet
Thoughts and Beliefs to Watch Out For

1. If my child respected me, he/she would listen to me.

2. A child who does not listen is disrespectful.

3. A child <u>does not have the right</u> to disagree with or challenge his or her father.

4. A child <u>should not</u> disagree with his or her father.

5. Children who disobey or who confront and challenge their father are being disrespectful and should be punished.

6. My child is ... stubborn, stupid, defiant, spoiled, etc.

7. If my child really cared about my feelings, he/she would....

8. My child should know better by now - he or she is doing this to get me.

9. My child is just like, or is acting just like, my ...(mother, father, brother, or some other family member).

10. If I don't get control of this situation, my child is going to turn into a ... (deadbeat, criminal, drug addict, etc).

11. I shouldn't have to deal with this situation right now.

12. If my child's mother would just ...... than this wouldn't happen.

Session 8 Homework

Identify two times that you were frustrated or upset with your child this week. What was the event and what were you thinking?

Describe a situation in the last week when you were frustrated or upset with your child.

_____

_____

_____

_____

_____

_____

What were you thinking at that time?

_____

_____

_____

_____

_____

_____

Describe a second situation in the last week when you were frustrated or upset with your child.

_____

_____

_____

_____

_____

What were you thinking at that time?

_____

_____

_____

_____

_____

_____

Session 8 Homework
Weekly Fathering Log

Name: _____ Week of: _____

This week, things I felt good about as a father were:

_____

_____

_____

Three ways that I praised my child this week:

(Be as specific as possible. What did you say?)

_____

_____

_____

_____

_____

This week, things I struggled with as a father were:

_____

_____

_____

_____

_____

If I were to rate how I felt about my parenting this past week on a scale of 1-5, where 1 means I did not feel good at all about the parenting choices I made and 5 means I felt great, my week was:

_____

Session 9
Developmental Charts

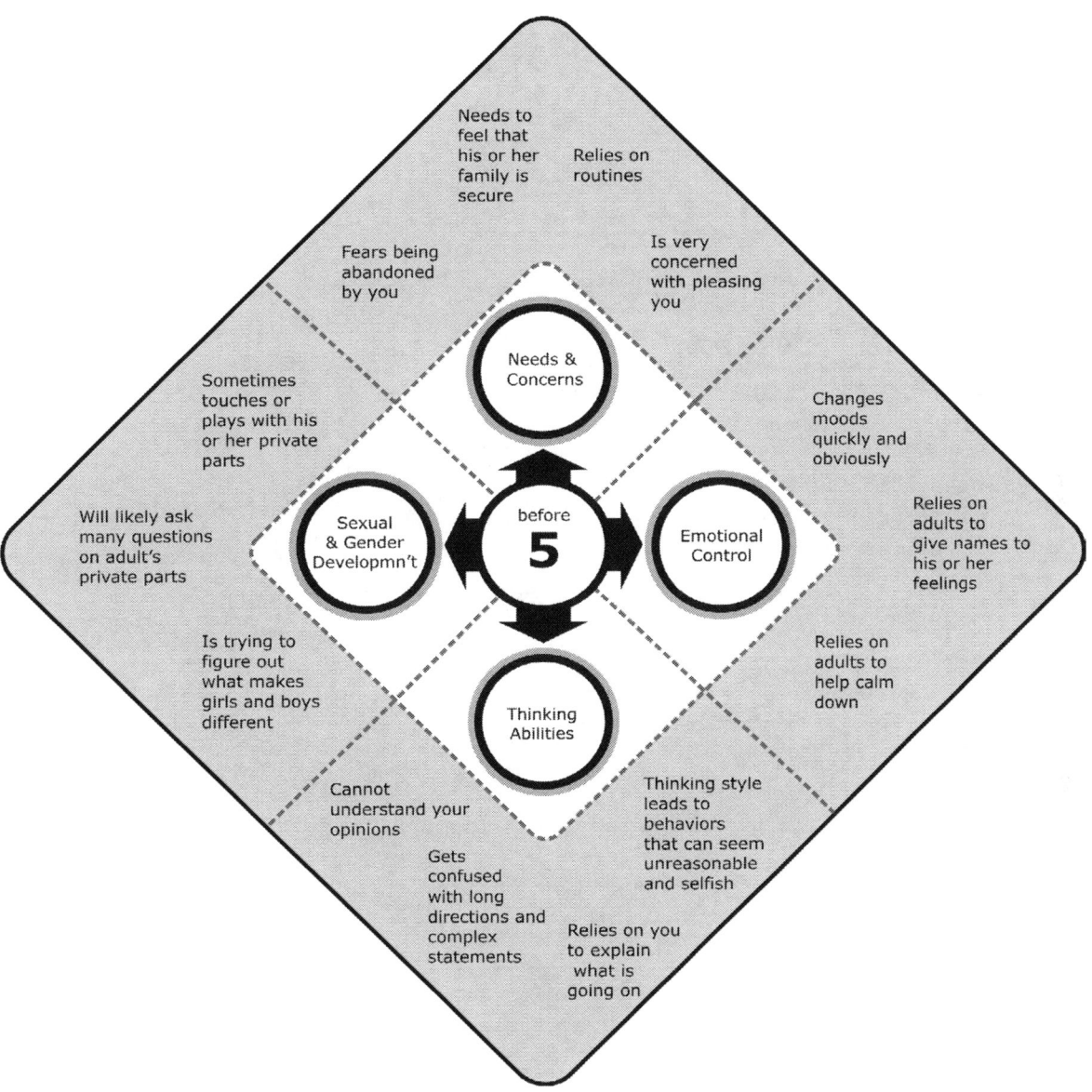

Needs to feel that his or her family is secure

Relies on routines

Fears being abandoned by you

Is very concerned with pleasing you

Sometimes touches or plays with his or her private parts

Needs & Concerns

Changes moods quickly and obviously

Will likely ask many questions on adult's private parts

Sexual & Gender Developmn't

before 5

Emotional Control

Relies on adults to give names to his or her feelings

Is trying to figure out what makes girls and boys different

Thinking Abilities

Relies on adults to help calm down

Cannot understand your opinions

Thinking style leads to behaviors that can seem unreasonable and selfish

Gets confused with long directions and complex statements

Relies on you to explain what is going on

Session 9
Developmental Charts

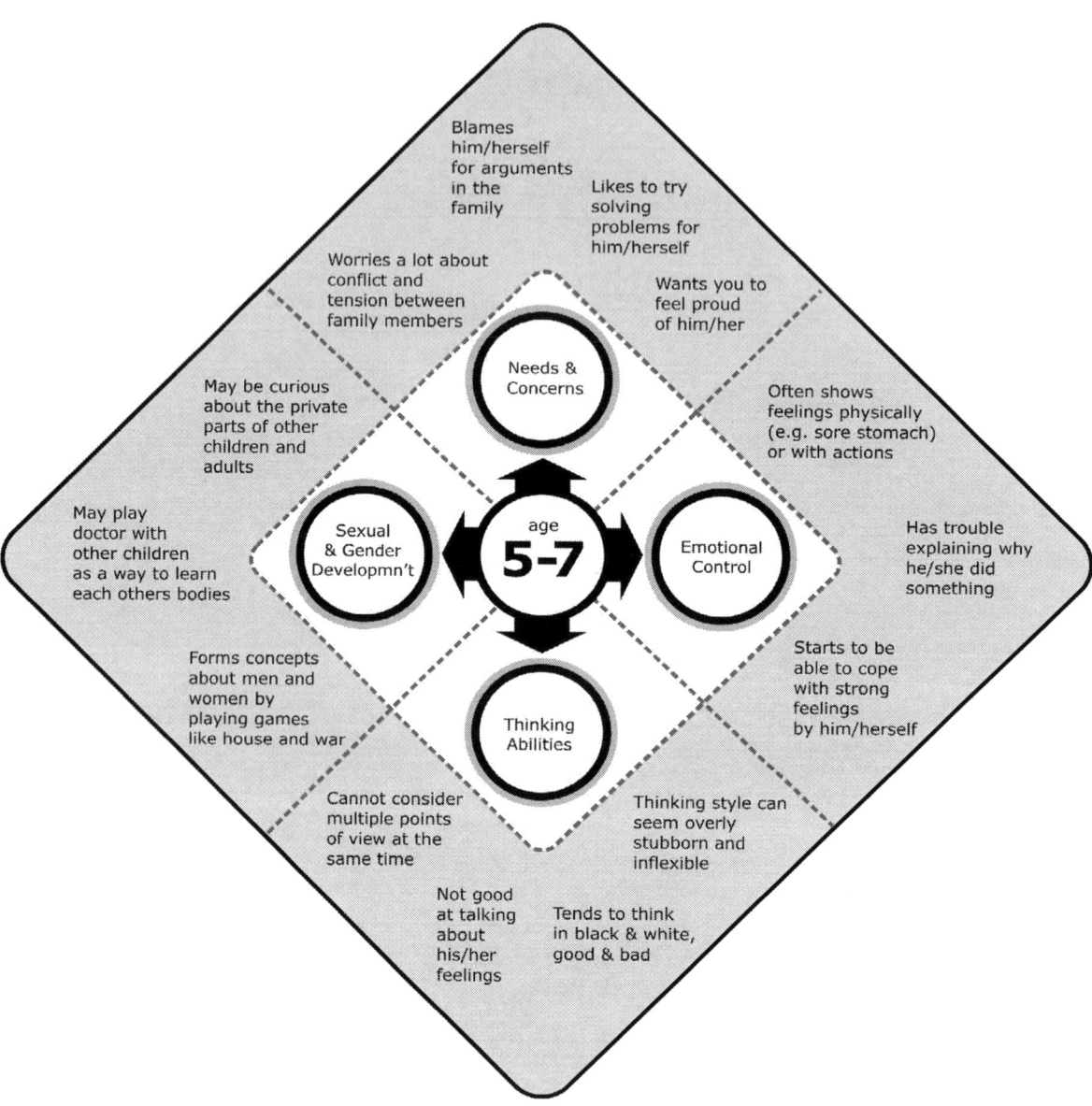

Blames him/herself for arguments in the family

Likes to try solving problems for him/herself

Worries a lot about conflict and tension between family members

Wants you to feel proud of him/her

May be curious about the private parts of other children and adults

Often shows feelings physically (e.g. sore stomach) or with actions

Needs & Concerns

May play doctor with other children as a way to learn each others bodies

Sexual & Gender Developmn't

age 5-7

Emotional Control

Has trouble explaining why he/she did something

Forms concepts about men and women by playing games like house and war

Thinking Abilities

Starts to be able to cope with strong feelings by him/herself

Cannot consider multiple points of view at the same time

Thinking style can seem overly stubborn and inflexible

Not good at talking about his/her feelings

Tends to think in black & white, good & bad

Session 9
Developmental Charts

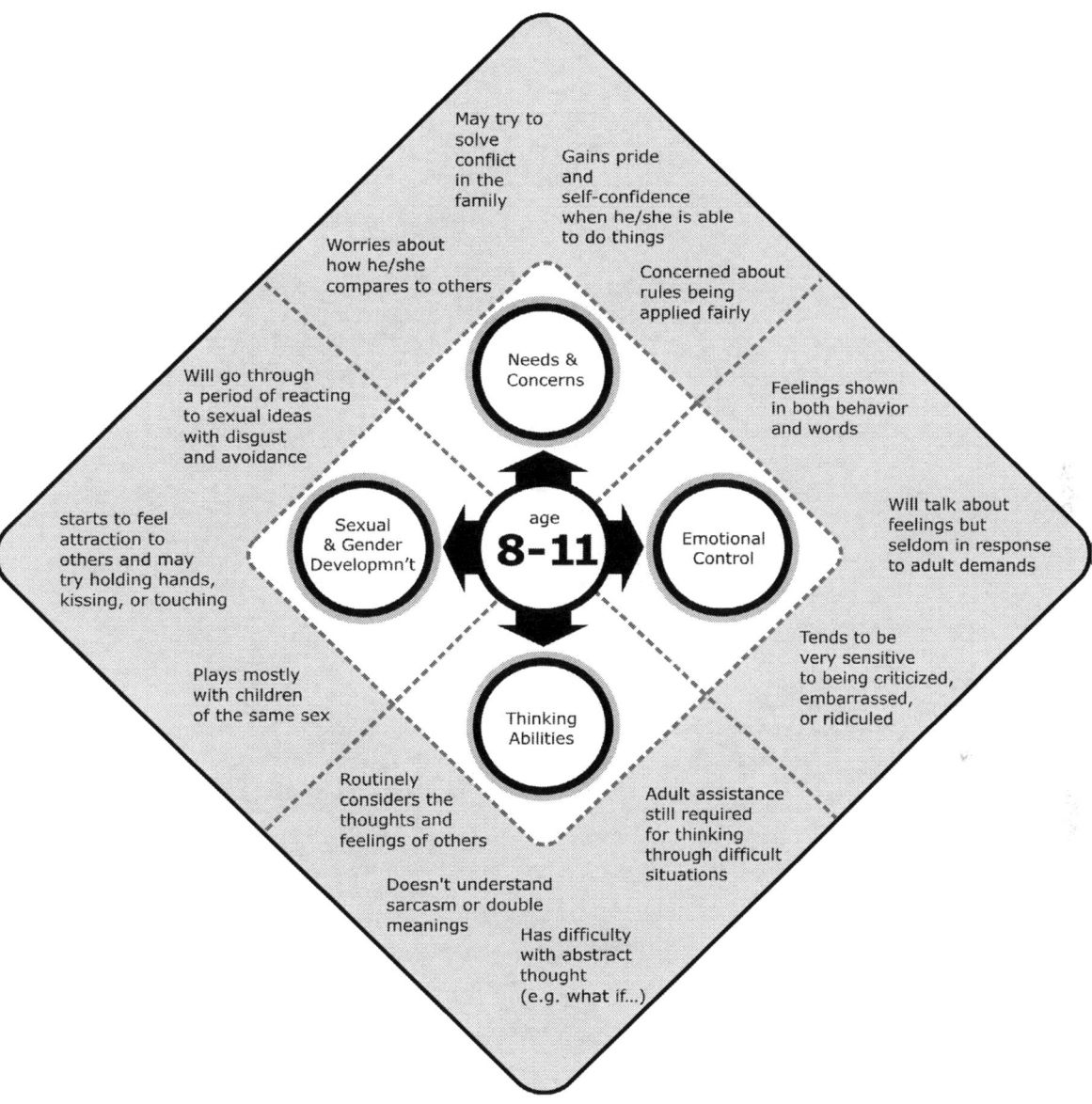

May try to solve conflict in the family

Gains pride and self-confidence when he/she is able to do things

Worries about how he/she compares to others

Concerned about rules being applied fairly

Will go through a period of reacting to sexual ideas with disgust and avoidance

Feelings shown in both behavior and words

Needs & Concerns

starts to feel attraction to others and may try holding hands, kissing, or touching

Sexual & Gender Developmn't

age 8-11

Emotional Control

Will talk about feelings but seldom in response to adult demands

Plays mostly with children of the same sex

Thinking Abilities

Tends to be very sensitive to being criticized, embarrassed, or ridiculed

Routinely considers the thoughts and feelings of others

Adult assistance still required for thinking through difficult situations

Doesn't understand sarcasm or double meanings

Has difficulty with abstract thought (e.g. what if...)

Session 9
Developmental Charts

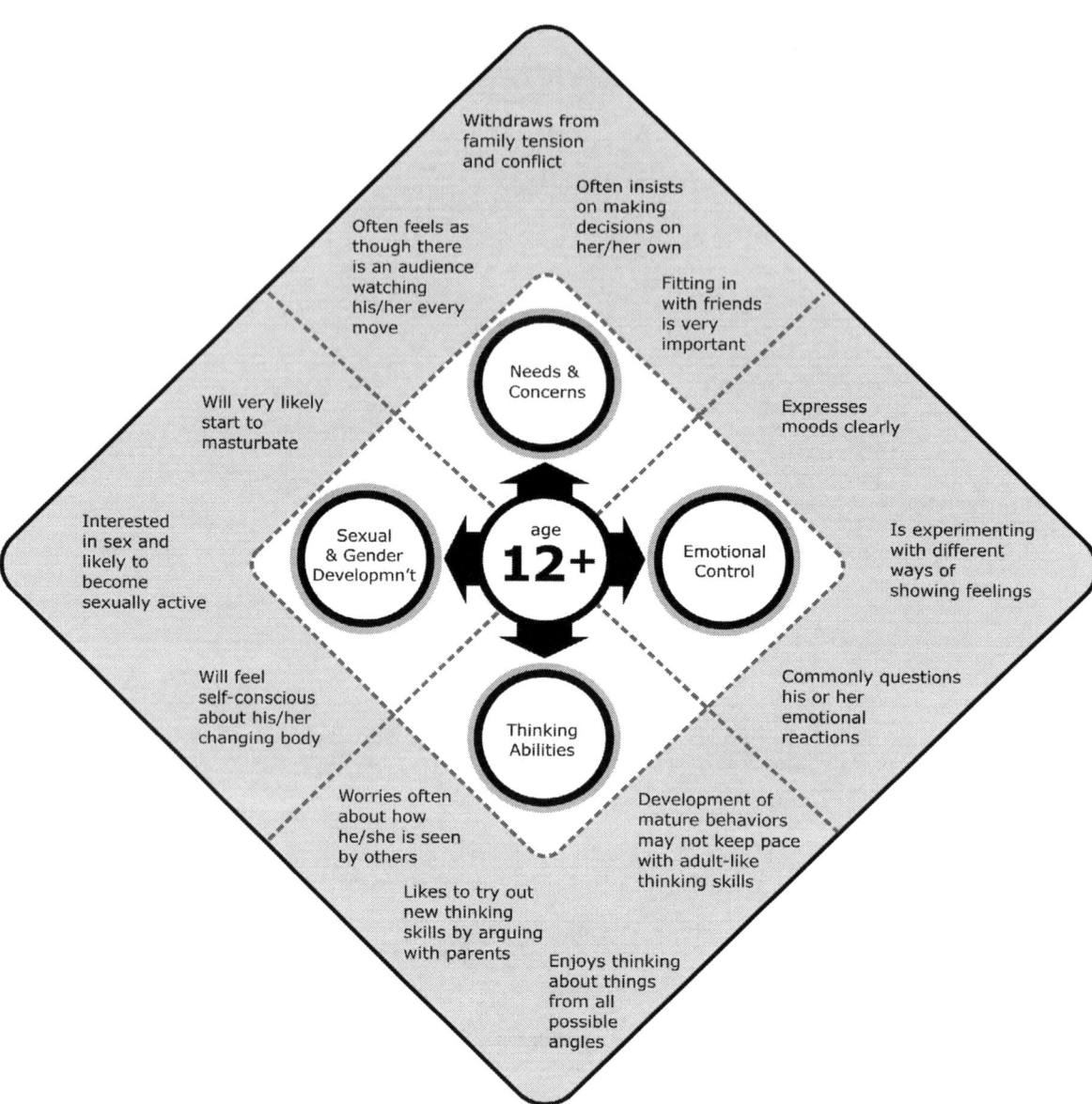

Session 9 Worksheet
Exercise 2: Practical Applications

Developmental Stage: Before Age 5

Common Parenting Situations:

1. Roger is embarrassed by, and finds himself getting angry with, his 18-month-old who always takes toys from other children in the playground and does not share when children come to visit at their house. He thinks to himself, "My child is very selfish".

2. John can't believe that his two-year-old says no all the time. It doesn't even seem to matter what is going on, the most likely word to come out of his child's mouth is no. He thinks: "Why does my child always have to disagree with me?"

3. Rob does not understand why his 3-year-old is so cranky and has been crying off-and-on all day. He let her stay up with him to watch a TV show when she refused to go down for her nap and he has been trying to do fun activities with her instead of following her typical routine. He thinks: "I really can't do anything right with this child".

4. Bill sees his 4-year-old on weekends. He finds it frustrating that his child gets upset every time they part. Each time, Bill explains that he will see his child again in one week but his child still gets upset. He thinks: "My child must really hate being at his mother's".

5. Stan feels left out. He has been working long hours and only gets to see his 14 month-old son Karl for a couple of hours each day. During that time he notices Karl often ignores him and runs crying to his mother. He thinks to himself: "She is already turning him into a momma's boy. Soon I will have no influence over him at all".

Session 9 Worksheet
Exercise 2: Practical Applications

Developmental Stage: 5 to 7-year-olds

Common Parenting Situations:

1. Fred is growing frustrated with his 5-year-old who becomes very upset when he and his wife so much as look at each other the wrong way. He would understand if they yelled at each other all the time in front of her but they don't and still she quickly picks up on whether they are in a disagreement and gets upset by this. Fred thinks: "My wife has turned my daughter against me".

2. Bob thinks that he should teach his 6-year-old son how to lose with grace by beating him at some games they play together. His son gets very upset when he loses and Bob is annoyed by this and thinks of his son as a sore loser.

3. Chris doesn't like the fact that his 7-year-old wants to have a say in deciding what the family is going to do on the weekend. Chris doesn't think his son should have so much control and feels that including his son is a waste of time, as his plans are not well thought-out.

4. Jim's 6-year-old has just returned home from school crying. Jim tried to talk to her but she wouldn't tell him what happened or how she was feeling. Jim thinks: "My child must not trust me".

5. Tim and Sue are going through a difficult time in their marriage and Tim finds himself yelling at Sue most nights. When their daughter Karen hears them fighting, she comes into the room and starts to cry for him to stop yelling at her mother. Tim thinks to himself: "Sue has already poisoned my own daughter against me."

Session 9 Worksheet
Exercise 2: Practical Applications

Developmental Stage: 8 to 11-year-olds

Common Parenting Situations:

1. Tom just finished telling his 10-year-old to stop playing with the stereo equipment and his child looks at him defiantly, says, "I do so know how to use this" and walks toward the equipment again. Tom thinks: "He is constantly defying me like this!"

2. Every time Rick asks his 9-year-old why he did something he shouldn't have, his child answers, "I dunno." Rick thinks: "He must think I am an idiot, or something".

3. Scott's 10-year-old daughter bursts into tears and storms to her room at the slightest teasing from him. Scott thinks: "She's such a big baby."

4. Pete thought he was being kind by offering to help his 11-year-old when she was having trouble making a card for her mother on the computer. Instead of a thank-you, she became angry with him and said she didn't need his help, she could do it herself. Pete thinks: "Since you don't appreciate it, this is last time I offer to help you!"

5. Charles' daughter Mary skipped by him on the way to the mall to meet her friends. Charles was angry because he had told her and her mother, Jolene, over and over again that no daughter of his was going to be caught hanging around at the mall. Charles thinks: "Mary and her mother are perfectly alike. They are both always trying to go against me".

Session 9 Worksheet
Exercise 2: Practical Applications

Developmental Stage: 12 Years and Older

Common Parenting Situations:

1. For the fourth time, Mark has told his 14-year-old that she cannot go to a dance that some of her older friends are attending. Even after explaining the reasons, she continues to argue her case. Mark thinks: "She doesn't respect our rules".

2. Tim is separated from his wife and likes to see his children whenever he can. He is hurt by the fact that his 15-year-old chooses to spend time with his friends rather than with his dad.

3. Tony's daughter used to hug and kiss him all the time but, since she turned 13, he is feeling rejected by her and doesn't understand why she is not affectionate with him anymore. He thinks: "She must have a boyfriend."

4. At times, Chad feels like kicking his 16-year-old out of the house. He sleeps too much, doesn't clean up after himself, can be really happy one day and really sad and angry the next, and argues with him all the time about his political and religious beliefs. Chad thinks: "I have had it with this kid. He doesn't appreciate a single thing that I do for him. He is just using us for room and board."

5. Shawn is convinced that his wife Leslie is having an affair. Although he has no proof, each night he questions her about where she has been and what she has been doing. Shawn's son Adam has started to step into these fights and defend his mother. In fact, just the other night, Adam told Shawn that he should "mind his own business and stop asking his mother all these questions." Shawn thinks: "What does he think he is doing anyway. This is between me and his mother and it's none of his business".

Session 9 Homework
Weekly Fathering Log

Name: _____ Week of: _____

This week, things I felt good about as a father were:

_____

_____

_____

Three ways that I praised my child this week:

(Be as specific as possible. What did you say?)

_____

_____

_____

_____

_____

This week, things I struggled with as a father were:

_____

_____

_____

_____

_____

If I were to rate how I felt about my parenting this past week on a scale of 1-5, where 1 means I did not feel good at all about the parenting choices I made and 5 means I felt great, my week was:

_____

Session 10
Not Valuing Children Wheel

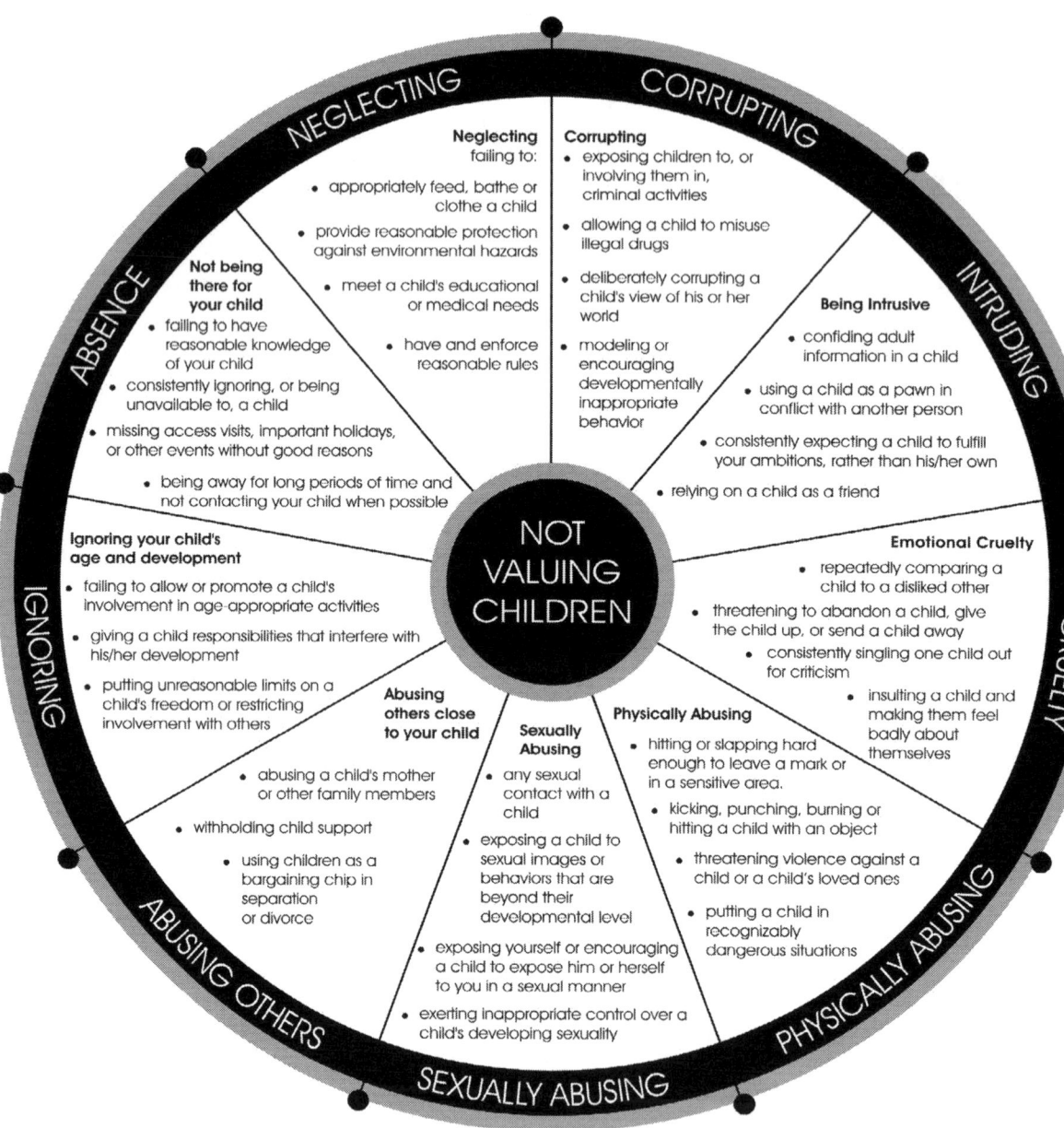

Neglecting
failing to:
- appropriately feed, bathe or clothe a child
- provide reasonable protection against environmental hazards
- meet a child's educational or medical needs
- have and enforce reasonable rules

Not being there for your child
- failing to have reasonable knowledge of your child
- consistently ignoring, or being unavailable to, a child
- missing access visits, important holidays, or other events without good reasons
- being away for long periods of time and not contacting your child when possible

Ignoring your child's age and development
- failing to allow or promote a child's involvement in age-appropriate activities
- giving a child responsibilities that interfere with his/her development
- putting unreasonable limits on a child's freedom or restricting involvement with others

Corrupting
- exposing children to, or involving them in, criminal activities
- allowing a child to misuse illegal drugs
- deliberately corrupting a child's view of his or her world
- modeling or encouraging developmentally inappropriate behavior

Being Intrusive
- confiding adult information in a child
- using a child as a pawn in conflict with another person
- consistently expecting a child to fulfill your ambitions, rather than his/her own
- relying on a child as a friend

Emotional Cruelty
- repeatedly comparing a child to a disliked other
- threatening to abandon a child, give the child up, or send a child away
- consistently singling one child out for criticism
- insulting a child and making them feel badly about themselves

Abusing others close to your child
- abusing a child's mother or other family members
- withholding child support
- using children as a bargaining chip in separation or divorce

Sexually Abusing
- any sexual contact with a child
- exposing a child to sexual images or behaviors that are beyond their developmental level
- exposing yourself or encouraging a child to expose him or herself to you in a sexual manner
- exerting inappropriate control over a child's developing sexuality

Physically Abusing
- hitting or slapping hard enough to leave a mark or in a sensitive area.
- kicking, punching, burning or hitting a child with an object
- threatening violence against a child or a child's loved ones
- putting a child in recognizably dangerous situations

NEGLECTING · CORRUPTING · INTRUDING · CRUELTY · PHYSICALLY ABUSING · SEXUALLY ABUSING · ABUSING OTHERS · IGNORING · ABSENCE

NOT VALUING CHILDREN

Session 10 Homework

List three things that you do that fall at the parent-centered end of the continuum. If you disagree a lot with your child's mother, try to think of one example from this relationship when your behavior has not been child-centered.

1. _____

2. _____

3. _____

Session 10 Homework
Weekly Fathering Log

Name: _____ Week of: _____

This week, things I felt good about as a father were:

_____

_____

_____

Three ways that I praised my child this week:

(Be as specific as possible. What did you say?)

_____

_____

_____

_____

_____

This week, things I struggled with as a father were:

_____

_____

_____

_____

_____

If I were to rate how I felt about my parenting this past week on a scale of 1-5, where 1 means I did not feel good at all about the parenting choices I made and 5 means I felt great, my week was:

_____

Session 11 Homework
Problem Solving for Parents

What is the situation?

_____

_____

_____

What was your intention?

_____

_____

_____

Is this about parent needs or child needs?

What were you feeling? _____

What did you do?   What were you thinking?

_____   _____

_____   _____

_____   _____

What was the effect on your child?

_____

_____

What could you have thought and done instead?

_____

_____

Session 11 Homework
Weekly Fathering Log

Name: _____ Week of: _____

This week, things I felt good about as a father were:

_____

_____

_____

Three ways that I praised my child this week:
(Be as specific as possible. What did you say?)

_____

_____

_____

_____

_____

This week, things I struggled with as a father were:

_____

_____

_____

_____

_____

If I were to rate how I felt about my parenting this past week on a scale of 1-5, where 1 means I did not feel good at all about the parenting choices I made and 5 means I felt great, my week was:

_____

Session 12

Myths and Facts: How Children are Affected by Parental Conflict

MYTH	*My child doesn't even know what's going on when we're fighting.*

FACT   Children *do* know that their parents are in conflict. They may see their father hit their mother, or throw or destroy objects. They may hear their father threaten their mother, or give her the "silent treatment." Even if they are not in the room, they can hear yelling, screaming, crying and slapping. They witness the after-effects of the abuse, such as a swollen lip, black eye, mom being "sick", or belongings destroyed.

MYTH	*Parental conflict has no real effect on children – they are not involved.*

FACT   Parental conflict is one of the strongest predictors of childhood problems. Children are even more damaged when parental conflict involves their father's abuse of their mothers. When this occurs, children may feel terrified for themselves and their mothers, anxious that it will happen again, afraid that they will be taken away, helpless to do anything, and angry at both parents. They may be hurt physically while trying to protect their mother. They may experience learning disruptions, speech and language problems, attention and behavior problems, and stress-related physical ailments (sleep problems, headaches, rashes, stomachaches). They may be too ashamed or feel too "different" to interact with other children, or may be too aggressive or hostile in their interactions with peers since that is what they've learned.

MYTH *My child may be upset for a little while, but s/he'll get over it soon enough.*

FACT Witnessing abuse has long-term effects on children. Children who have witnessed domestic violence are at greater risk for anxiety, depression, alcohol/drug abuse and juvenile delinquency, bullying, and violence in later relationships.

MYTH *My children know that they shouldn't hit. My "infrequent" acts of violence won't change that.*

FACT Children learn by what their parents do, not what they say. Boys who witnessed domestic violence while growing up are more likely to abuse their female partners than boys who didn't witness domestic violence.

MYTH *My children know that our fights are not their fault.*

FACT Children often feel guilty in response to their parents' conflicts. They may feel that they caused the abuser to become angry, and thus the conflict is their fault, or that they should have stopped the abuse. They also may feel guilty for loving the abuser, or for siding with the victim.

MYTH *You can be a good father and a "bad" husband or "X".*

FACT When you hurt your child's mother, you hurt your child.

Session 12 Homework
Problem Solving for Parents

What is the situation?

_____

_____

_____

What was your intention?

_____

_____

_____

Is this about parent needs or child needs?

What were you feeling? _____

What did you do?   What were you thinking?

_____   _____

_____   _____

_____   _____

What was the effect on your child?

_____

_____

What could you have thought and done instead?

_____

_____

Session 12 Homework
Weekly Fathering Log

Name: _____ Week of: _____

This week, things I felt good about as a father were:

_____

_____

_____

Three ways that I praised my child this week:

(Be as specific as possible. What did you say?)

_____

_____

_____

_____

_____

This week, things I struggled with as a father were:

_____

_____

_____

_____

_____

If I were to rate how I felt about my parenting this past week on a scale of 1-5, where 1 means I did not feel good at all about the parenting choices I made and 5 means I felt great, my week was:

_____

Session 13 Worksheet

What Children Learn From Abusive and Controlling Fathering

1. Children learn that it's acceptable to use violence to deal with disagreements, and that it's okay to hit someone if they don't agree with what that person is saying or doing.

2. Children learn that hitting is a good way to make someone stop doing something they don't like, or to make someone do something s/he doesn't want to do.

3. Children learn that others have the control - especially bigger stronger others. They do not learn that they can make decisions themselves, that they are capable of doing so.

4. Children learn that love and violence go together. This sets the stage to accept violence in other relationships.

5. Children learn that when someone is under stress, tense or angry, violence is an acceptable way to cope.

6. Children learn that they deserve to be hit if they have done something that the other person disapproves of.

7. Children learn to deal with other authority figures, like teachers, in unhealthy ways.

8. Children learn not to get caught.

9. Children learn to avoid the person who has abused them, and they lose trust in that person. They learn that this person is not safe and cannot be relied upon to help them.

Session 13 Homework
Problem Solving for Parents

What is the situation?

_____

_____

_____

What was your intention?

_____

_____

_____

Is this about parent needs or child needs?

What were you feeling? _____

What did you do?   What were you thinking?

_____   _____

_____   _____

_____   _____

What was the effect on your child?

_____

_____

What could you have thought and done instead?

_____

_____

Session 13 Homework
Weekly Fathering Log

Name: _____ Week of: _____

This week, things I felt good about as a father were:

_____

_____

_____

Three ways that I praised my child this week:

(Be as specific as possible. What did you say?)

_____

_____

_____

_____

_____

This week, things I struggled with as a father were:

_____

_____

_____

_____

If I were to rate how I felt about my parenting this past week on a scale of 1-5, where 1 means I did not feel good at all about the parenting choices I made and 5 means I felt great, my week was:

_____

Session 14 Homework
Weekly Fathering Log

Name: _____ Week of: _____

This week, things I felt good about as a father were:

_____

_____

_____

Three ways that I praised my child this week:

(Be as specific as possible. What did you say?)

_____

_____

_____

_____

_____

This week, things I struggled with as a father were:

_____

_____

_____

_____

If I were to rate how I felt about my parenting this past week on a scale of 1-5, where 1 means I did not feel good at all about the parenting choices I made and 5 means I felt great, my week was:

_____

Session 15
Talking to Children About Violence

Benefits of Talking to Kids About Violence

- Children learn that violence isn't their fault.

- Children learn that violence isn't an acceptable way to solve problems.

- It helps children feel cared for and understood.

- Children learn that it's okay to talk about feelings.

- Children learn (by example) to take responsibility for their behavior.

What Children Need to Hear You Say

- It's not your fault.

- I will listen to you.

- I am sorry that you saw/heard/experienced that. What I did was not OK.

- I am sorry that something I did made you feel worried, hurt, or unsafe.

- There is nothing you could have done to prevent/change it.

- You can tell me how you feel; how you feel is important.

- We can talk about what to do to keep you feeling safe.

- You do not deserve to have this in your family.

- What happened was not okay. I should not have done what I did.

- It must have been scary for you.

Session 15 Homework

List one or two problems that still occur in your relationship with your children. Be as specific as possible.

1._____

_____

_____

2._____

_____

_____

What strategies do I have to cope with these difficulties in a more child-centered manner? In other words, how can I respond to these difficulties in a different way?

_____

_____

_____

_____

_____

Session 15 Homework
Weekly Fathering Log

Name: _____ Week of: _____

This week, things I felt good about as a father were:

_____

_____

_____

Three ways that I praised my child this week:

(Be as specific as possible. What did you say?)

_____

_____

_____

_____

_____

This week, things I struggled with as a father were:

_____

_____

_____

_____

If I were to rate how I felt about my parenting this past week on a scale of 1-5, where 1 means I did not feel good at all about the parenting choices I made and 5 means I felt great, my week was:

_____

Session 16 Handout
Alternative Methods of Child Management

1. Consider what things I can live with. Can I change my demands?

2. How can I arrange the situation so that this argument doesn't come up?

3. How can I encourage/support my child's positive behaviors?

4. Is there a natural consequence or an outside authority that I can rely on?

5. What is child misbehavior really about? Can I fix that problem?

Session 16 Homework
Weekly Fathering Log

Name: _____ Week of: _____

This week, things I felt good about as a father were:

_____

_____

_____

Three ways that I praised my child this week:

(Be as specific as possible. What did you say?)

_____

_____

_____

_____

_____

This week, things I struggled with as a father were:

_____

_____

_____

_____

If I were to rate how I felt about my parenting this past week on a scale of 1-5, where 1 means I did not feel good at all about the parenting choices I made and 5 means I felt great, my week was:

_____

Session 16 Homework
How Have I Done?

At the beginning of *Caring Dads*, you identified hopes and goals for your relationship with your children. Review these hopes and goals and comment on how you have progressed over the group.

_____

_____

_____

_____

_____

_____

_____

_____

Homework: Alternative Parenting Steps

List three things that you have learned from this group. How have these lessons helped you become a better parent?

1._____

_____

_____

2._____

_____

_____

3._____

_____

_____

APPENDIX B:

Program Eligibility Criteria, Service Agreement and Group Rules Samples

Appendix B

Program Eligibility Criteria Sample

Many fathers are likely to benefit from participation in this program, but in particular, we are seeking men who use over-controlling, physically or emotionally abusive, and/or neglectful parenting strategies. Appropriate referrals include, but are not limited to, men who:

- Have physically or emotionally abused their children
- Are at-risk for maltreating their children
- Have an overbearing, controlling style of interacting with their children
- Are alternatively over-involved and distant with their children
- Have physically or emotionally abused children's mothers

Men also need to:

- Have regular involvement in caring for their children (i.e. at least every other week access)
- Have at least one child between the ages of 0 and 12
-

Men are not eligible for the *Caring Dads* group if they:

- Have a history of perpetration of child sexual abuse
- Are actively and currently involved in a custody and access dispute
- Have no regular contact with their children
- Are on an Early Intervention Conditions

Please note that individual suitability for the group will also be assessed through a clinical intake process.

Service Agreement Sample

Program Commitment

We commit to providing you with a program that is designed to help you think carefully about how you relate to your children. We will work with you to change parenting practices that are harmful and to develop skills to improve your relationship with your children.

We will provide you with open and honest assessments about your behavior and will make appropriate referrals and recommendations if needed.

We will treat you with respect.

We will be honest about your participation and progress.

Suggestions for changes and improvement of services and complaints or grievances may be expressed to your group co-facilitators. If necessary, you may then contact _____ who will forward your comments for discussion at working group meetings.

Confidentiality

Your identity and written and oral statements will be kept confidential with the following exceptions:

- if there are reasonable grounds to suspect child abuse, a report will be made to child protective services
- if you make threats or gestures of harm towards yourself or others, it will be reported to the appropriate persons and/or authorities
- if disclosure is required by Court Order or subpoena

As part of our commitment to treat you with respect, we will, to the best of our ability, inform you if we feel the need to break confidentiality.

In addition, program co-facilitators will maintain open communication with your referral agents (i.e., child protective services and probation and parole).

Communication

If you share custody, the mother of your children and children that you regularly care for will be given general information about the *Caring Dads* program. She will also be provided with support and resources, if she chooses. This contact is in the best interests of your children, and we require that you do not interfere with this contact or use it against the mother of your children.

In the case that the mother of your children contacts *Caring Dads* during your involvement with this program, we will share with her general information about the *Caring Dads* program (e.g. number of weeks, content of session). We will need your consent to share any information with her about your particular involvement in this group.

The *Caring Dads* program does not provide letters of support to men, their lawyers or other professionals. Once you have begun the program, a letter will be sent to your referral agent indicating that you have enrolled in the program. Regular updates on your attendance will be provided, upon request, to your referral agent. Once you have completed the program, a final report will be sent to your referral agent.

If you become involved in regularly caring for additional children while you are in the program, you are asked to provide the name and contact information for the mother of these children to program co-facilitators.

The *Caring Dads* program requires you to sign request Release of Information consent forms for communication between *Caring Dads* and your referral agent. If you share custody of your children, you will also be required to consent for release of the name and contact information of the mother of your children. If you are involved with other professionals, you may be asked to sign additional consent and release of information forms.

Advisory about Program Completion

Program completion does not guarantee that you will improve your parenting. Developing better parenting skills depends upon your own behavior and commitment. The final report made to your referral agent will reflect the judgments of your group facilitators about your participation and learning in group.

Limits of Involvement

You are expected to report to group co-facilitators any criminal behavior (e.g., assault, stalking, breach of restraining order, breach/violation of probation or custody and access agreements, failing to make child support payments), regardless of who the offence was against or whether the criminal justice system was involved. Co-facilitators will work with you to ensure behaviors are reported to the proper authorities.

You are expected to abstain from using alcohol and recreational drugs 24 hours prior to group meetings. Any man who arrives at group having used such substances will be asked to leave the meeting. You should inform your group co-facilitator if you are taking prescriptions drugs that alter your emotions or behavior (e.g., anti-depressant, anti-psychotic, sedatives). You may be asked to sign a release of information so that the purpose of this prescription can be discussed with your physician.

You are expected to wear appropriate clothing. You will be asked to obscure (e.g. by turning a shirt inside out) or remove any clothing viewed by group co-facilitators as racist, sexist or otherwise disrespectful.

You are not permitted to enter group premises with weapons of any kind.

You are expected to be respectful of others in the group by maintaining others' confidentiality and using respectful language.

Persistent or gross disregard of any of the above rules may be addressed in a number of ways. You may be asked to develop an agreement with your co-facilitators and/or other authorities for more appropriate behavior (this is most often the first step). The program may impose additional conditions on your continued participation in group. Finally, you may be asked to leave the program.

Other Rules

Smoking is not permitted anywhere in the building. Smoking is permitted outside of the building at the front door. You will be allowed re-entrance by a group facilitator.

Cellular telephones and paging devices must be turned off during group. Personal telephone calls are permitted in cases of emergency.

Attendance and Participation

The fathering program runs one night a week for 17 weeks. You are expected to attend all sessions but are permitted to miss a maximum of two sessions for documented reasons (e.g. family emergencies, sickness). If you are going to miss a session (or if you have missed a session), you need to call _____ to let your facilitators know. You will need to collect handouts and complete homework from missed sessions. If you miss more than two sessions, you will be discharged from the program.

You may not miss consecutive sessions without permission from group co-facilitators.

Meetings start promptly at the scheduled time and run for two hours. In general, men who arrive late will not be admitted into the group.

Groups do not run on statutory holidays. In cases of unexpected inclement weather, you should call _____ for information about whether or not group is cancelled.

You are expected to participate actively in group discussions, to accept challenges, and to challenge others respectfully.

You are expected to complete all homework assignments. You will be considered to have completed the program only when your homework assignments are completed and have been checked by a group facilitator.

Group Rules Sample

1. Keep confidentiality within the group. When discussing group activities, focus only on your contribution.

2. Maintain respectful behavior toward everyone in the meetings.

3. Use first names when speaking to other group members or when making reference to women or children in your life.

4. Do not use alcohol or drugs in the 24 hours prior to your meeting.

5. Active participation in group is required.

6. Meetings begin sharply at the scheduled time.

7. Always bring your workbook.

8. Stay focused on the meeting theme.

ISBN 141205709-4

9 781412 057097